The Gen X Series

IMO International Mathematics Olympiad **NSO** National Science Olympiad **NCO** National Cyber Olympiad **IEO** International English Olympiad

OLYMPIAD SAMPLE PAPERS 7

Useful for Olympiads Conducted at School, National & International Levels

Compiled By
Editorial Board

Strictly According to the Latest Syllabus of Olympiad

V&S PUBLISHERS

Published by:

F-2/16, Ansari road, Daryaganj, New Delhi-110002
☎ 23240026, 23240027 • *Fax:* 011-23240028
Email: info@vspublishers.com • *Website:* www.vspublishers.com

Regional Office : Hyderabad
5-1-707/1, Brij Bhawan (Beside Central Bank of India Lane)
Bank Street, Koti, Hyderabad - 500 095
☎ 040-24737290
E-mail: vspublishershyd@gmail.com

Branch Office : Mumbai
Jaywant Industrial Estate, 1st Floor–108, Tardeo Road
Opposite Sobo Central Mall, Mumbai – 400 034
☎ 022-23510736
E-mail: vspublishersmum@gmail.com

BUY OUR BOOKS FROM: AMAZON FLIPKART

© Copyright: V&S PUBLISHERS

ISBN 978-93-579423-2-4
New Edition

DISCLAIMER

While every attempt has been made to provide accurate and timely information in this book, neither the author nor the publisher assumes any responsibility for errors, unintended omissions or commissions detected therein. The author and publisher makes no representation or warranty with respect to the comprehensiveness or completeness of the contents provided.

All matters included have been simplified under professional guidance for general information only, without any warranty for applicability on an individual. Any mention of an organization or a website in the book, by way of citation or as a source of additional information, doesn't imply the endorsement of the content either by the author or the publisher. It is possible that websites cited may have changed or removed between the time of editing and publishing the book.

Results from using the expert opinion in this book will be totally dependent on individual circumstances and factors beyond the control of the author and the publisher.

It makes sense to elicit advice from well informed sources before implementing the ideas given in the book. The reader assumes full responsibility for the consequences arising out from reading this book.

For proper guidance, it is advisable to read the book under the watchful eyes of parents/guardian. The buyer of this book assumes all responsibility for the use of given materials and information.

The copyright of the entire content of this book rests with the author/publisher. Any infringement/transmission of the cover design, text or illustrations, in any form, by any means, by any entity will invite legal action and be responsible for consequences thereon.

Publisher's Note

The current decade has firmly established V&S Publishers as one of the Leading Publishers of General Trade Mass Appeal Books across popular genres along with Academic Books for School Children. Having been in publishing trade for over 40 years, we understand the need of the hour when it comes to Books. After successfully publishing around 600 titles in the last decade and establishing a pan India network of booksellers & distributors including ecommerce platforms – Amazon, Flipkart etc; we determined after a nation-wide market research in tier 1, 2 and 3 cities that preparatory materials for status-acquiring OLYMPIAD BOOKS is the need of the hour.

And in true spirit, the Olympiad books on Science, Maths, English and Cyber published for classes 1 to 10 was picked by students off the shelf in no time. It acquired the 'Bestseller' image. Encouraged by this huge acceptability of our Olympiad Series among parents, students and booksellers alike, we at V&S Publishers decided to take PREPARATION to the next level by bringing out another handholding masterpiece – Olympiad Sample Papers.

These Sample Papers are the virtual replicas of the actual exam papers.

Yes! These Sample Papers are the virtual replicas of the actual exam papers. Inclusion of two sets each for Science, Maths, English and Cyber subjects from classes 1 to 10 in respective books are believed to be adequate to prepare students mentally for 'live exam conditions.' Anything else would have been 'under-preparation' or over-preparation'

You will hardly be able to differentiate the Sample Papers from the Actual Exam Papers. All this has been made possible by the people who have been in their respective fields for years – coaching and guiding students to succeed in this vital exam.

P.S. While every care has been taken to ensure correctness of content, if you come across any error, howsoever minor, anywhere in the book, do not hesitate to discuss with your teachers while pointing that out to us in no uncertain terms.

We wish you All the Best!

Contents

INTERNATIONAL MATHEMATICS OLYMPIAD (IMO)

Mock Test Paper 1

Total Questions : 50 Time : 1 Hour

PATTERN AND MARKING SCHEME				
Section	(1) Logical Reasoning	(2) Mathematical Reasoning	(3) Everyday Mathematics	(4) Achievers Section
No. of Questions	15	20	10	5
Marks per Questions	1	1	1	3

SYLLABUS

Section – 1: Verbal and Non-Verbal Reasoning

Section – 2: Integers, Fractions and Decimals, Exponents and Powers, Algebraic Expressions, Simple Linear Equations, Lines and Angles, Comparing Quantities, The Triangle and its Properties, Symmetry, Congruence of Triangles, Rational Numbers, Perimeter and Area, Data Handling, Visualizing Solid Shapes, Practical Geometry.

Section – 3: Syllabus as per Section– 2.

Section – 4: Higher Order Thinking Questions – Syllabus as per Section – 2.

LOGICAL REASONING

1. There is a certain relationship between the given pair of figures. Identify the relationship and find the missing figure.

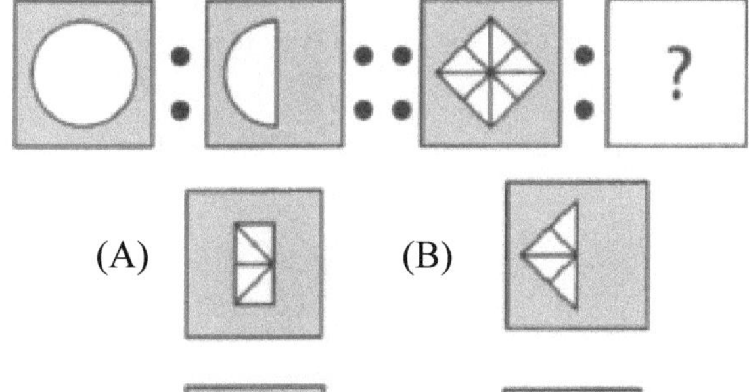

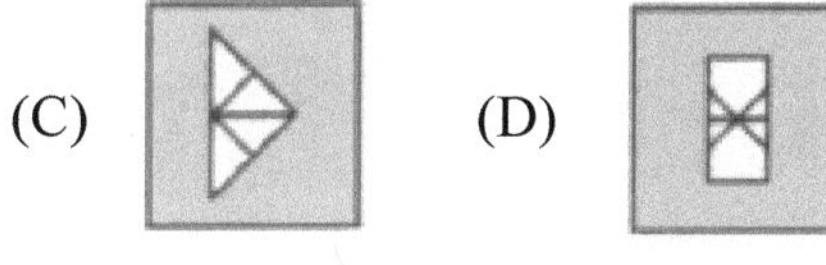

2. Pointing towards Kanika, Ashish said, "The son of her only brother is the brother of my wife." How is Kanika related to Ashish?

   (A) Mother
   (B) Sister of father-in-law
   (C) Sister
   (D) Maternal Aunt

3. If PAINT is coded as 74128 and EXCEL is coded as 93596, then how would you encode ACCEPT?

   (A) 812356 (B) 124967
   (C) 658942 (D) 455978

4. Vihaan started to walk straight towards south. After walking 5 m he turned to the left and walked 3 m. After this he turned to the right and walked 5 m. Now to which direction Vihaan is facing?

   (A) West
   (B) South
   (C) North
   (D) None of these

5. If the alphabet series is arranged in reverse order, which letter will be twelfth to the left of the fourteenth letter from your left?
   (A) T (B) F
   (C) Y (D) S

6. If P denotes 'multiplied by', T denotes 'subtracted from', Y denotes 'added to' and Z denotes 'divided by, then find the value of 28Z7P8T6Y4.
   (A) 12 (B) 22
   (C) 30 (D) 24

7. Select the one which satisfies the same conditions of placement of the dot(s) as in the figure (X).

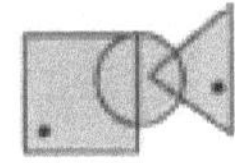

Fig. (X)

(A)  (B) 

(C)  (D) 

8. Choose one figure from the options that resembles the unfolded form of the fig. Z.

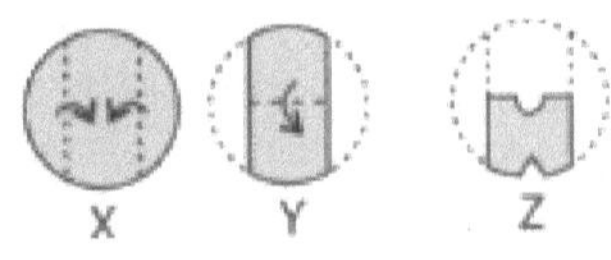

(A) (B)

(C) (D)

9. Count the number of cubes in the given figure.

   (A) 8 (B) 14
   (C) 10 (D) 16

10. Find out which figure in given options completes the figure matrix.

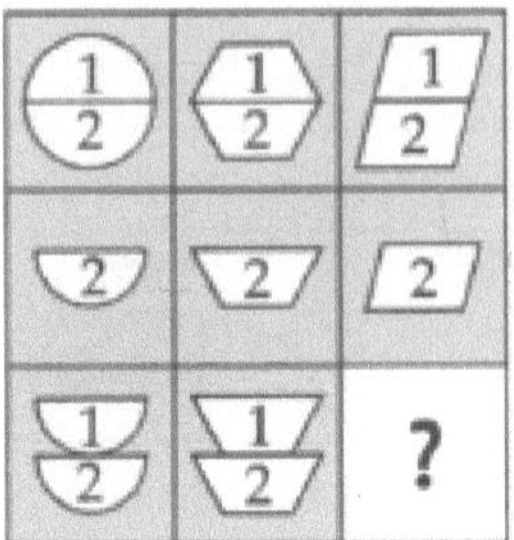

(A) (B)

(C) (D)

11. Fig. (X) is exactly embedded in any one of the options. Find the option which contains fig. (X) as one of its part.

Fig. (X)

(A) (B) 

(C) (D)

12. Choose the correct water image of the given figure (X) from the given options.

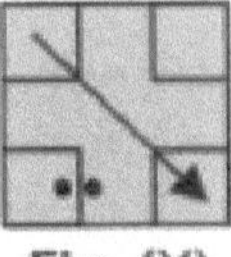

Fig. (X)

(A) 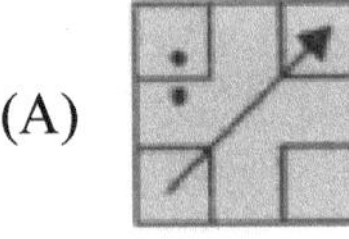 (B) 

 (C) 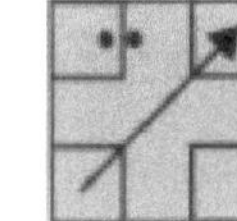 (D) 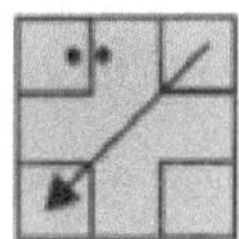

13. Count the minimum number of straight lines in the given figure.

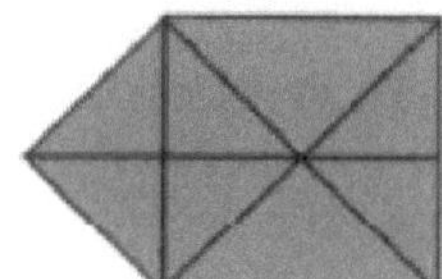

(A) 12 (B) 6
(C) 9 (D) 18

14. Choose odd one out.

 (A)   (B) 

(C)   (D) 

15. Which number will replace the question mark?

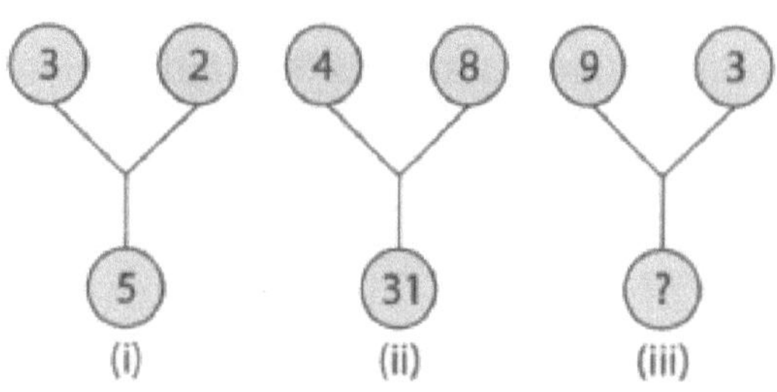

(A) 26 (B) 25
(C) 32 (D) 28

MATHEMATICAL REASONING

16. Simplify

$$\frac{\left(16a^{2}\right)^{\frac{1}{2}} \times \left(36a^{4}\right)^{\frac{-1}{2}}}{2a^{\frac{1}{2}} \times 5a^{\frac{3}{2}} \times 8a^{\frac{9}{4}}}$$

(A) $24a^{-25/4}$ (B) $120a^{25/4}$
(C) $24a^{25/4}$ (D) $\frac{1}{120a^{21/4}}$

17. The denominator of a fraction is 3 more than its numerator. If 2 is added to both the numerator and the denominator, the fraction becomes 2/3. What is the original fraction?
(A) 2/7 (B) 4/7
(C) 1/5 (D) 5/3

18. In the given figure, find the measure of $\angle RQT$, if PQ = QR and $\angle QPR = 60°$.

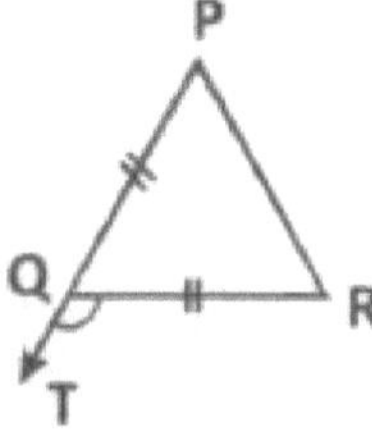

(A) 135°
(B) 120°
(C) 60°
(D) None of these

19. What is the place value of 3 in 9.365?
(A) 300 (B) 3/10
(C) 3 (D) 3/100

20. What is the value of x?

$$\frac{7}{8} - \left(-\frac{11}{4}\right) + x = 3\frac{7}{24}$$

(A) −1/3 (B) 3
(C) 2/3 (D) 1/3

21. What is the value of 124 × 4 − 3 + 118 ÷ 2?
(A) 825 (B) 496
(C) 552 (D) −553

22. Find the measure of y in the given figure.

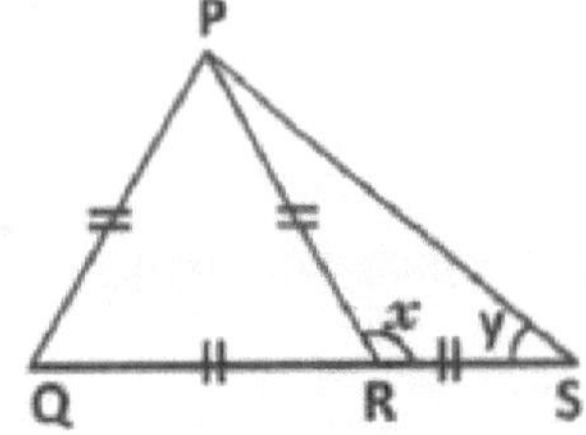

(A) 90° (B) 60°
(C) 30° (D) 120°

23. When a number is reduced by 4, it becomes 80% of itself. Find the number.
(A) 65 (B) 20
(C) 150 (D) 40

24. By selling an article for ₹ 600 a man loses 20%. At what price should he sell it in order to gain 25%?
(A) ₹ 937.50 (B) ₹ 650
(C) ₹ 725 (D) ₹ 1200

25. In a chemistry lab, there are 3 beakers for every 6 students. How many beakers will be required for 24 students?
(A) 16
(B) 8
(C) 12
(D) None of these

26. If 2A = 3B = 4C, what is the value of A : B : C?
(A) 3 : 4 : 6 (B) 4 : 2 : 1
(C) 6 : 4 : 3 (D) 1 : 3 : 4

27. If ₹ 85 amounts to ₹ 95 in 3 years, what will ₹ 102 amount to in 5 years at the same rate?
(A) ₹ 320 (B) ₹ 308
(C) ₹ 122 (D) ₹ 196

28. When a certain number, 'm' is divided by 5 and added to 8, the result is equal to thrice the number subtracted from 4. What is the value of 'm'?
(A) −4/3 (B) 1/3
(C) 4 (D) −5/4

29. ΔABC and ΔDEF are shown below.

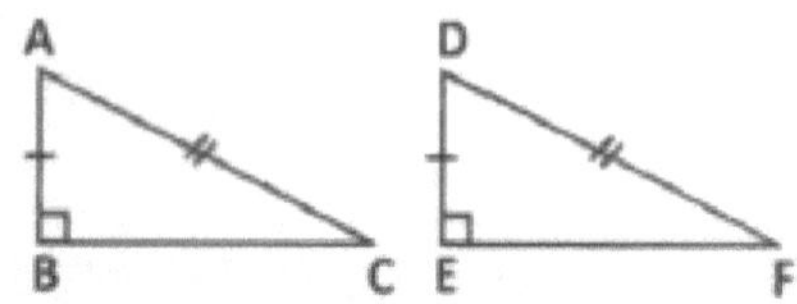

By which condition of congruence is ΔABC ≅ ΔDEF?
(A) RHS criterion
(B) SSS criterion
(C) ASA criterion
(D) AAS criterion

30. Shubham reads 1/3 part of a book in 1 hour. How much part of the book will he read in $2\frac{1}{5}$ hours?
(A) 1/15 (B) 11/15
(C) 25/12 (D) None of these

31. If the angles $(2x - 10)°$ and $(x - 11)°$ are complementary, what is the value of 'x'?
(A) 37° (B) 28°
(C) 12° (D) 9°

32. The mean of five numbers is 27. If one of the numbers is excluded, the mean gets reduced by 2. What is the excluded number?
(A) 28 (B) 35
(C) 15 (D) 20

33. Which of the following figures has rotational symmetry of order more than 1?

(A) 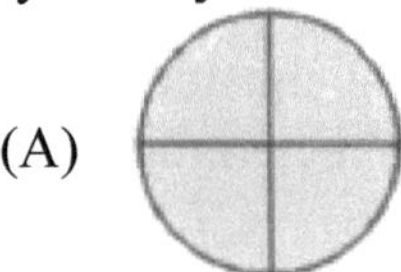

(B) 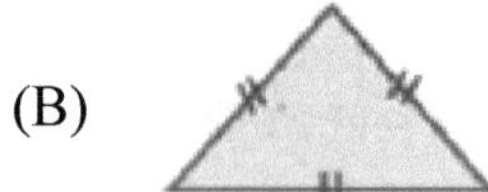

(C) 

(D) All of these

34. A wire bent in the form of a circle of radius 42 cm is again bent in the form of a square. What is the ratio of the regions enclosed by the circle and the square?
(A) 21 : 33 (B) 22 : 33
(C) 14 : 11 (D) 11 : 12

35. Which of the given objects has exactly two flat faces?
(A) 
(B) 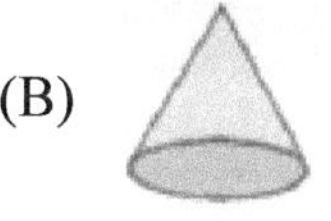
(C) 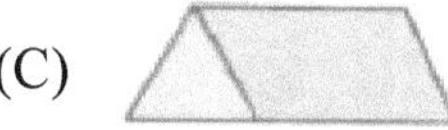
(D) 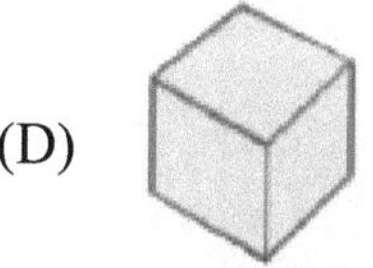

EVERYDAY MATHEMATICS

36. A fruit basket has 23 mangoes and apples . How many apples are there in the basket if there are '*p*' mangoes in it?
(A) $23p$
(B) $23-p$
(C) $23+p$
(D) None of these

37. In an election between two candidates, the candidate who gets 30% of the votes polled is defeated by 15000 votes. What is the number of votes polled for the winning candidate?
(A) 37500 (B) 30000
(C) 26250 (D) 11250

38. A building is 24 m long. The bottom of the ladder is 10 m away from the foot of the building. Find the length of the ladder ?
(A) 22 m (B) 28 m
(C) 26 m (D) 18 m

39. If Mahima gives an interest of ₹ 45 for one year at 9% rate p.a. What is the sum she has borrowed?
(A) ₹ 400 (B) ₹ 650
(C) ₹ 1500 (D) ₹ 500

40. Sonia sells a washing machine for ₹ 13,500. She loses 20% in the bargain. What was the price at which she bought it?
(A) ₹ 17500 (B) ₹ 15000
(C) ₹ 16875 (D) ₹ 14400

41. Shubham reads 3/5 of a book. He finds that there are still 80 pages left to be read. What is the total number of pages in the book?
(A) 100 (B) 200
(C) 300 (D) 400

42. How many pieces of equal size can be cut from a ribbon of length 30 m, each measuring $3\frac{3}{4}$ metres?
(A) 20 (B) 24
(C) 12 (D) 8

43. A man walked 3 km towards North, then 8 km towards South. What is his final position with respect to his initial position?
(A) 5 km towards South
(B) 8 km towards North
(C) 5 km towards East
(D) 3 km towards South

44. Gaurav has 96 marbles and Shobha has 63 marbles. How many marbles should Shobha give Gaurav so that Gaurav will have twice as many marbles as Shobha?
(A) 30 (B) 10
(C) 25 (D) 15

45. Anu had a rectangular plot measuring 500 m by 100 m. She wants to fence her plot. Find the cost of fencing at the rate of ₹ 150 per metre.
(A) ₹ 150000 (B) ₹ 180000
(C) ₹ 66000 (D) ₹ 48000

46. If p, q and r are positive integers and $p+\cfrac{1}{q+\cfrac{1}{r}}=\frac{25}{19}$, find the value of q.

(A) $p=1, q=3, r=6$
(B) $p=2, q=1, r=4$
(C) $p=5, q=2, r=1$
(D) $p=6, q=0, r=2$

47. Find the perimeter of the given figure.

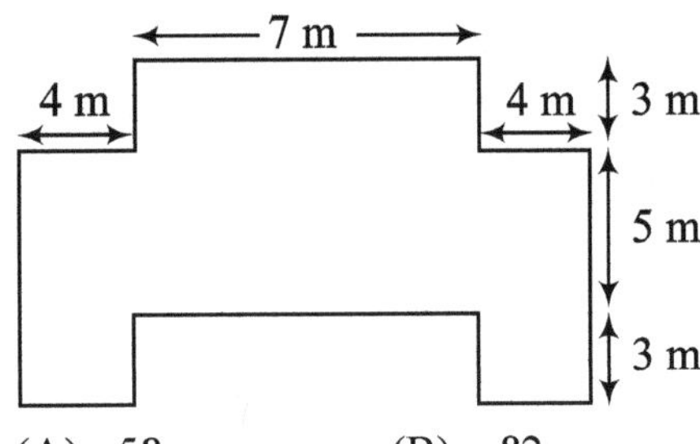

(A) 58 cm (B) 82 cm
(C) 96 cm (D) 48 cm

48. The average weight of a sample of 10 apples is 52 g. Later it was found that the weighing machine had shown the weight of each apple 10 g less. What is the correct average weight of an apple?

(A) 62 g (B) 45 g
(C) 52 g (D) 82 g

49. The minute hand of a circular clock is 14 cm long. How far does its tip move in 1 hour?

(A) 196 cm (B) 94.2 cm
(C) 28 cm (D) 88 cm

50. Find the measure of x in the following figure.

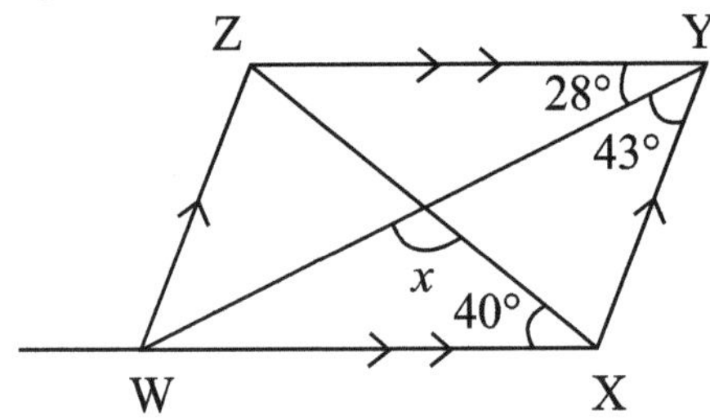

(A) 65° (B) 112°
(C) 68° (D) 96°

Mock Test Paper 2

I M O

INTERNATIONAL MATHEMATICS OLYMPIAD

Total Questions : 50 Time : 1 Hour

PATTERN AND MARKING SCHEME				
Section	**(1) Logical Reasoning**	**(2) Mathematical Reasoning**	**(3) Everyday Mathematics**	**(4) Achievers Section**
No. of Questions	15	20	10	5
Marks per Questions	1	1	1	3

SYLLABUS

Section – 1: Verbal and Non-Verbal Reasoning

Section – 2: Integers, Fractions and Decimals, Exponents and Powers, Algebraic Expressions, Simple Linear Equations, Lines and Angles, Comparing Quantities, The Triangle and its Properties, Symmetry, Congruence of Triangles, Rational Numbers, Perimeter and Area, Data Handling, Visualizing Solid Shapes, Practical Geometry.

Section – 3: Syllabus as per Section– 2.

Section – 4: Higher Order Thinking Questions – Syllabus as per Section – 2.

LOGICAL REASONING

1. Select a figure from the options, which will continue the same series as established by the Problem Figures.

Problem Figures

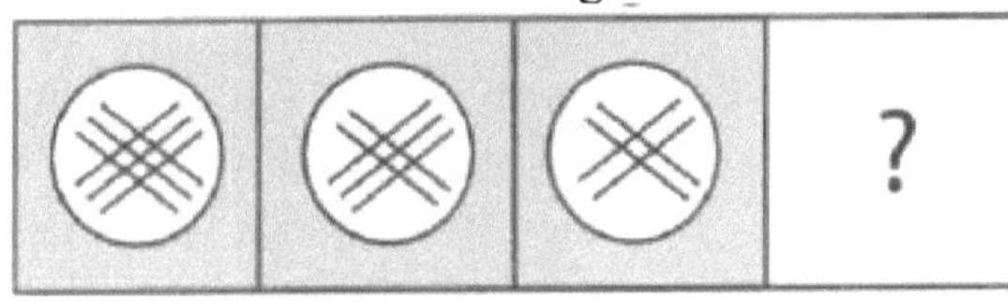

(A) 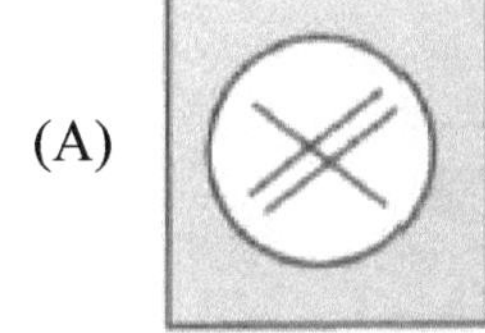

(B) 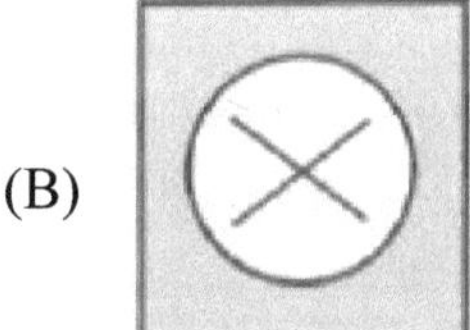

(C) 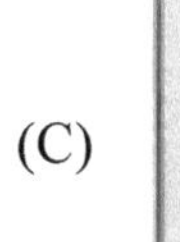 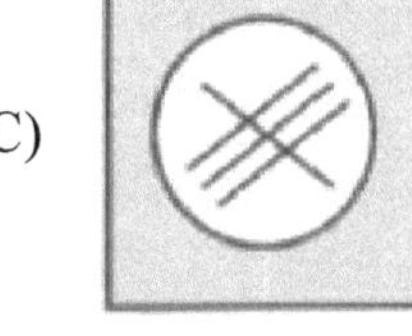

(D) 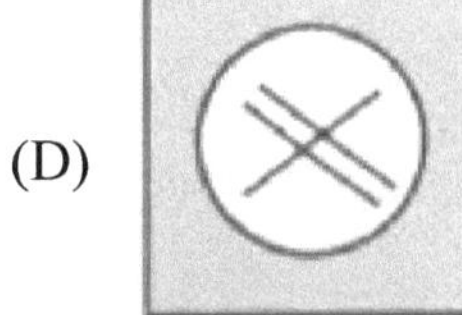

2. Choose the figure which is different from others.

(A) 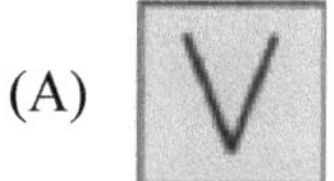 (B) 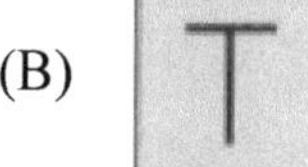

(C) 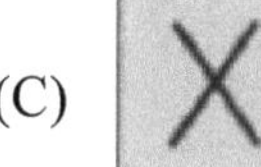 (D) 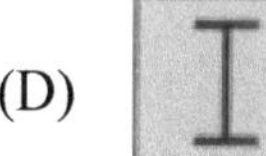

3. Count the number of rectangles in the given figure.

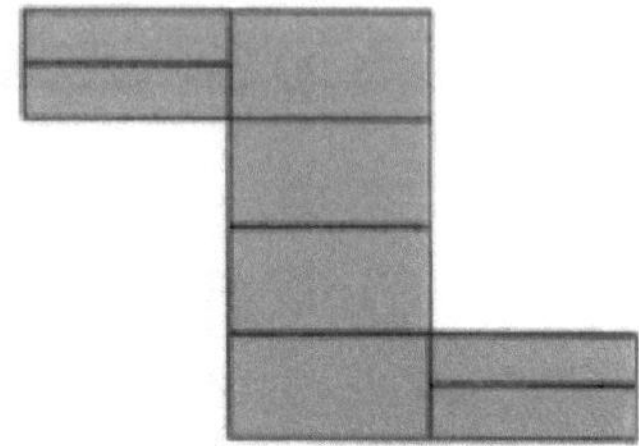

(A) 12 (B) 15
(C) 10 (D) 14

4. If the first day of a month is Monday, which of the following will be the fifth day from 21st of the month ?

(A) Tuesday (B) Saturday
(C) Friday (D) Monday

5. If '+' denotes '–' , '–' denotes '×', '×' denotes '÷', and '÷' denotes '+', then find the value of $15 \times 3 \div 15 + 5 - 2$.

(A) 16 (B) 10
(C) 0 (D) 12

6. Study the diagram and identify the people who can speak only one language.

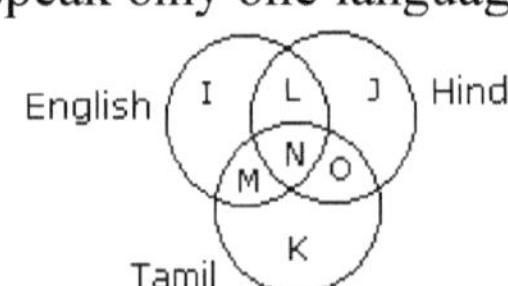

(A) K + J + I
(B) L + O + M
(C) M + N + L
(D) None of these

7. In certain code language, MILD is coded as NKOH, then how will GATE be coded in that language?

(A) HCWI
(B) MSQP
(C) CTOR
(D) None of these

8. Pointing to Vinay, Esha says, "I am the daughter of the only son of his grandfather." How is Esha related to Vinay?

(A) Sister
(B) Aunt
(C) Grandmother
(D) Can't be determined

9. Study the two positions of a dice given below. What number will be on the top if 4 is at the bottom?

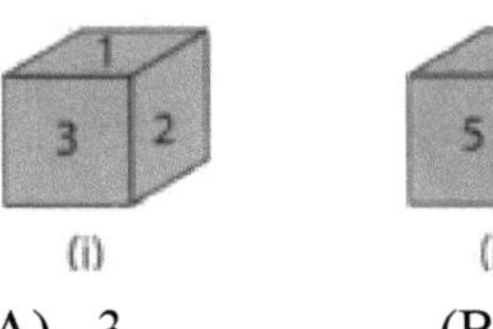

(i) (ii)

(A) 3 (B) 4
(C) 1 (D) 5

10. Select a figure from the four options that has same conditions of the placement of the dots as in Fig. (X).

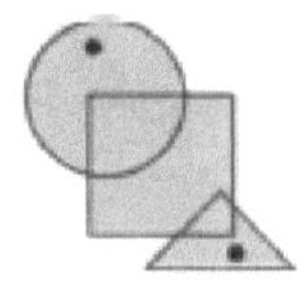

Fig. (X)

(A)  (B) 

(C) 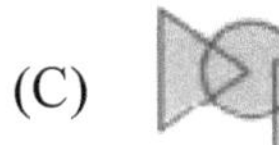  (D) 

11. Choose the correct figure from the four options which represents the sheet X after folding it along the dotted line.

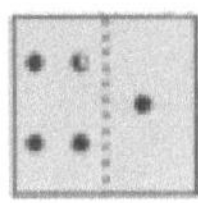

Sheet (X)

(A) 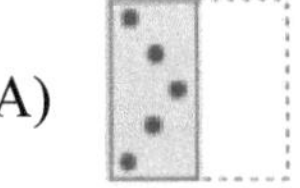 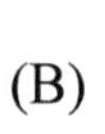 (B) 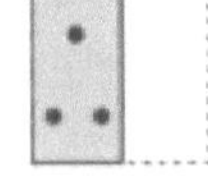

(C) 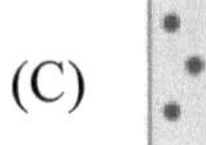 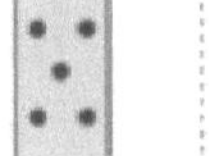 (D) 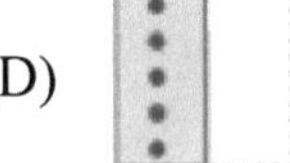

12. Find the missing figure in the given figure matrix.

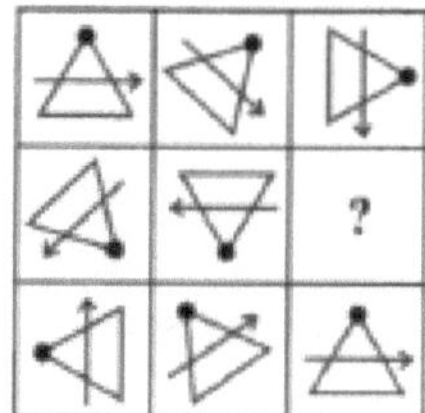

(A) (B)

(C) (D)

13. Choose a figure from the four options that exactly embeds the figure (X).

Fig. (X)

(A) 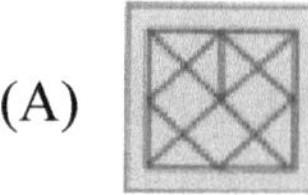 (B) 

(C)  (D) 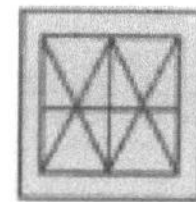

14. Choose the mirror image of fig (X).

Fig. (X)

(A)  (B) 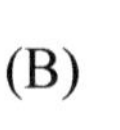 

(C)   (D)  

15. Complete the given analogy.

180 : 18 : : ? : 16

(A) 80
(B) 120
(C) 160
(D) None of these

MATHEMATICAL REASONING

16. Identify the solid with 3 rectangular and 2 triangular faces.

(A) 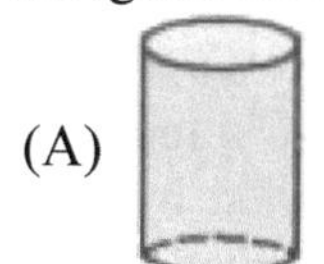

(B) 

(C) 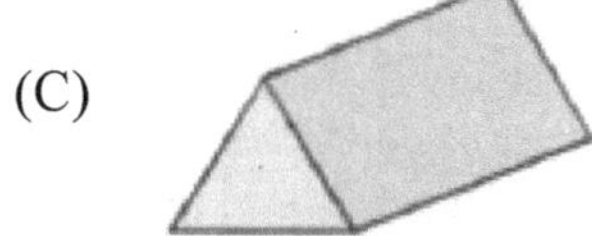

(D)

17. Evaluate

$$\frac{x-4}{3}-\frac{2x+1}{6}=\frac{5x+1}{2}$$

(A) 7/5 (B) 1/5
(C) 4/6 (D) −4/5

18. Which of the following figures has only one line of symmetry?

(A) 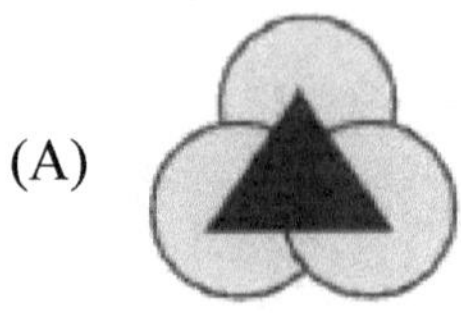

(B) 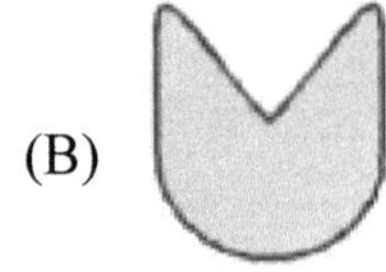

(C) 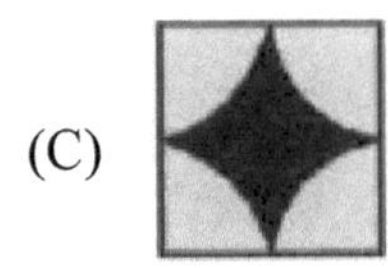

(D) 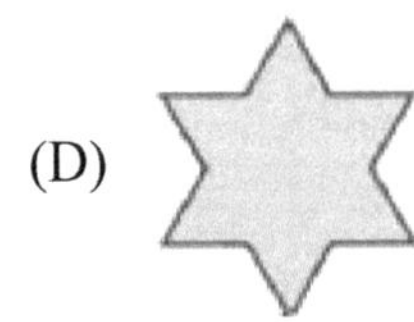

19. Diya has a box with 6 colored blocks numbered from 1 to 6 on each of them. She picks a block from it without seeing. What is the probability that the block picked has the number 3 on it?

(A) 1/6 (B) 4/3
(C) 3/4 (D) 5/4

20. PQR is a straight line.

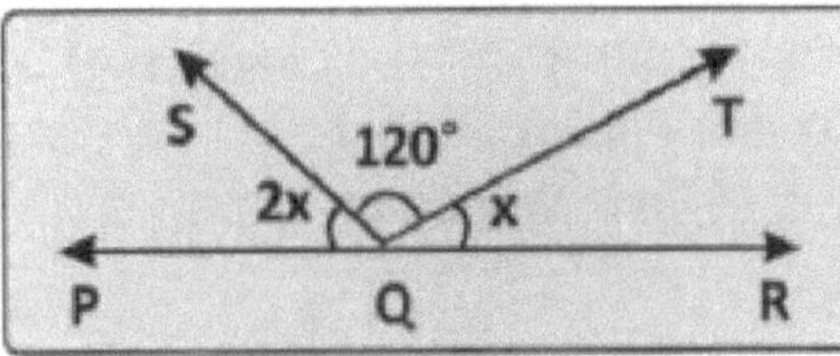

What is the value of x?

(A) 20° (B) 55°
(C) 25° (D) 60°

21. A car covers a distance of 89.1 km in 2.2 hours. What is the average distance covered by it in 1 hour?

(A) 32.2 km (B) 54.4 km
(C) 40.5 km (D) 68.6 km

22. In the given figure, AB = AC and AD is the bisector of ∠BAC.

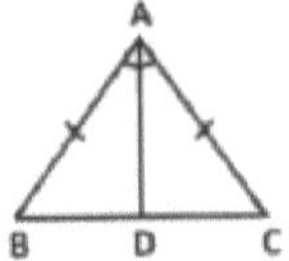

Which among the following statements is true?

(A) $\Delta ADC \cong \Delta ABC$
(B) $\Delta ADB \cong \Delta ABC$
(C) $\angle B = \angle C$
(D) $\angle ABC = \angle CAB$

23. What is the value of given expression
$\left(a^3 - 2a^2 + 4a - 5\right) - \left(-a^3 - 8a + 2a^2 + 5\right)$

(A) $4a^3 + 6a^2 + 11a - 12$
(B) $2a^3 - 5a^2 + 3a - 9$
(C) $2a^3 - 4a^2 + 12a - 10$
(D) None of these

24. A certain sum of money lent out at a certain rate of interest per annum, doubles itself in 10 years. In how many years will it triple itself?

(A) 12 years (B) 20 years
(C) 15 years (D) 9 years

25. If 20 : 5 :: *p* : 1, what is the value of *p*?

(A) 1 (B) 4
(C) 4/3 (D) 1/6

26. A student has to secure 40% marks to pass. He got 40 marks and failed by 40 marks. What is the maximum number of marks?

(A) 600 (B) 580
(C) 400 (D) 200

27. A contractor hired 120 men to build a wall in 45 days. After 15 days, he was joined by 30 more men. In how many days will the remaining work be finished?

(A) 24 days (B) 18 days
(C) 48 days (D) 20 days

28. The CP of 25 articles is equal to the SP of 20 articles. What is the gain%?

(A) 25% (B) 12.5%
(C) 28% (D) 10%

29. Find the value of x.

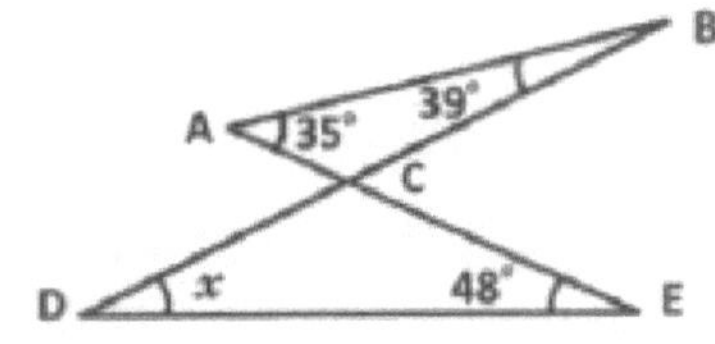

(A) 55° (B) 26°
(C) 68° (D) 112°

30. The product of two integers is −48. If one of the integers is −6, what is the value of the other?

(A) 4 (B) 288
(C) 1 (D) 8

31. The product of two rational numbers is −9/16. If one of the numbers is −4/3, what is the other number?

(A) 26/48 (B) 25/24
(C) 1/49 (D) 27/64

32. What is the value of

$$3\frac{1}{12}-\left[1\frac{3}{4}+\left\{2\frac{1}{2}-\left(1\frac{1}{2}-\frac{1}{3}\right)\right\}\right]$$

(A) 4 (B) 1.5
(C) 0 (D) 6

33. A triangle ΔPQR with ∠Q = 90°, QR = 8 cm and PR = 10 cm is constructed. What would be the measure of PQ?

(A) 8 cm (B) 10 cm
(C) 6 cm (D) 14 cm

34. The circular ring of radius 35 m is surrounded by a path of width 7 m around it on the outside. What is the area of the path?

(A) 1496 m^2 (B) 1265 m^2
(C) 1880 m^2 (D) 1694 m^2

35. Find the value of m.

$$\left(5^3\right)^m\times\left(5^8\right)^m=5^{72}$$

(A) $m=6$ (B) $m=15$
(C) $m=6\frac{6}{11}$ (D) $m=8$

EVERYDAY MATHEMATICS

36. Meena wants to put a lace on the edge of a circular table cover of diameter 28 m. Find the length of the lace required.

(A) 64 m (B) 120 m
(C) 88 m (D) 72 m

37. Vishal's father is 44 years old. If he is 5 years older than thrice Vishal's age. Which of these equations gives, the age of Vishal's father?

(A) $3x-5=44$
(B) $44=15x$
(C) $3x+5=44$
(D) None of these

38. Bhoomi reads a book for $1\frac{3}{4}$ hours every day. She reads the entire book in 6 days. How many hours in all were required by her to read the book?

(A) 25/4 hours
(B) $10\frac{1}{2}$ hours
(C) 35/3 hours
(D) None of these

39. Aman buys a recorder for ₹ 600 and sells it at a gain of 25%. At what price should he sell it?

(A) ₹ 720 (B) ₹ 940
(C) ₹ 1080 (D) ₹ 1200

40. Asha and Mohan borrowed ₹ 2250 and ₹ 2500 respectively at the same rate of simple interest for 3 years. If the interest paid by Mohan is ₹ 45 more than that paid by Asha, what is the rate of interest per annum?

(A) 7 % p.a. (B) 8 % p.a.
(C) 3 % p.a. (D) 6 % p.a.

41. 35% population of a town are men and 40% are women. If the number of children is 20,000, what is the number of women?

(A) 3200 (B) 32000
(C) 30050 (D) 31500

42. A scooter covers a distance of 55.3 km in one litre of petrol. How much distance will it cover in 10 litres of petrol?

(A) 553 km (B) 650 km
(C) 320 km (D) 850 km

43. In a class test containing 15 questions, 4 marks are given for every correct answer and (−2) marks are given for every incorrect answer. Manu attempts all questions but only 9 of her answers are correct. What is her total score?

(A) 20
(B) 24
(C) 28
(D) None of these

44. Akshat can run 100 metres in 13.5 seconds. If he competes in the 500 metres race, about how many seconds will it take him to run the race ?

(A) 40 secs (B) 50 secs
(C) 67.5 secs (D) 32 secs

45. 'y' packets of 8 pencils each are divided equally among 16 children. How many pencils does each child get?

(A) $24y$
(B) $8y$
(C) $y/2$
(D) None of these

ACHIEVERS SECTION

46. If ABCD is a rectangle having length 30 cm and breadth 20 cm, E, F and G are midpoints of AB, CD and AD respectively, find the area of the unshaded part.

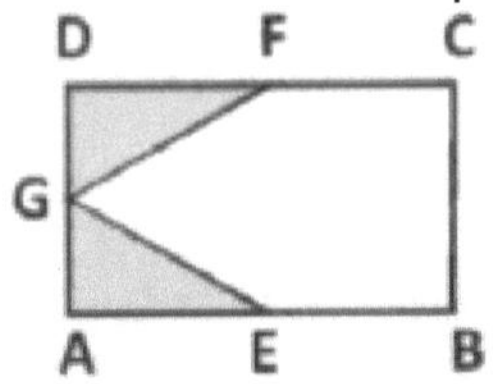

(A) 400 cm^2
(B) 375 cm^2
(C) 450 cm^2
(D) 600 cm^2

47. In the given figure, AB =AC and AD =AE.

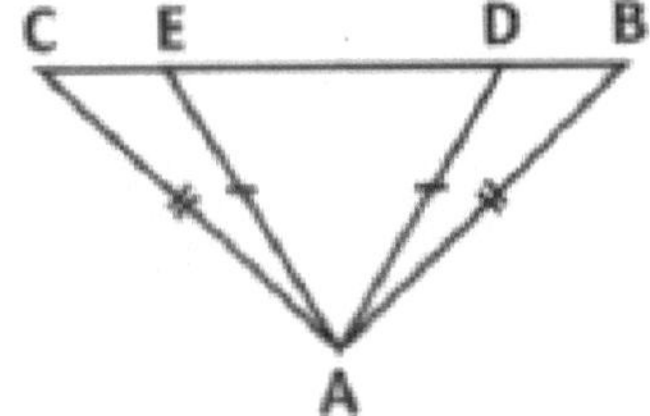

Which of the following statements is true?

(A) $\angle CAE = \angle BAD$
(B) BE = DC
(C) AE = CE
(D) $\Delta AEC \cong \Delta ADB$

48. Simplify

$$\frac{2\times 3^4 \times 2^5}{9\times 4^2}$$

(A) 12
(B) 36
(C) 24
(D) None of these

49. In a two digit number, the units digit is x and tens digit is $(x + 3)$. What is the sum of the digits in the number?

(A) $2x + 3$
(B) $11x + 3$
(C) $3 + x$
(D) $11x + 30$

50. Suppose that x and y are positive numbers with

$$xy = \frac{1}{9}$$

$$x(y+1) = \frac{7}{9}$$

$$y(x+1) = \frac{5}{18}$$

What is the value of $(x + 1)(y + 1)$?

(A) 16/25

(B) 35/18

(C) 42/18

(D) None of these

NATIONAL SCIENCE OLYMPIAD NSO

Mock Test Paper 1

N S O

NATIONAL SCIENCE OLYMPIAD

Total Questions : 50 Time : 1 Hour

PATTERN AND MARKING SCHEME			
Section	**(1) Logical Reasoning**	**(2) Science**	**(3) Achievers Section**
No. of Questions	10	35	5
Marks per Questions	1	1	3

SYLLABUS

Section – 1: Verbal and Non-Verbal Reasoning.

Section – 2: Heat, Motion and Time, Electric Current and its Effects, Winds, Storms and Cyclones, Light, Acids, Bases and Salts, Physical and Chemical Changes, Weather, Climate and Adaptations of Animals to Climate, Fibre to Fabric, Nutrition in Plants and Animals, Respiration in Organisms, Transportation in Plants and Animals, Reproduction in Plants, Natural Resources and Their Conservation (Soil, Water: A Precious Resource, Forests our Lifeline, Wastewater Story).

Section – 3: Higher Order Thinking Questions – Syllabus as per Section – 2.

LOGICAL REASONING

1. West: North- East :: South : ?
   (A) North- West
   (B) South- West
   (C) North- East
   (D) Cannot be predicted.

2. Kanika started driving and after moving 6 Kms she turned to her right and continued for 2 Kms. Then she turned to the left and drive for 10 Kms. In the end, she was moving towards the North side. Determine the direction which she was facing when she started moving.
   (A) South (B) East
   (C) West (D) North

3. **Statement:** All the girls are beautiful. Some girls are intelligent.
   Conclusion : All the girls are intelligent
   (A) All beautiful girls are intelligent.
   (B) Some beautiful girls are intelligent.
   (C) Conclusion is correct.
   (D) Cannot be determined.

4. Samiksha, Saba, Simran are three friends. The total of their ages is 70. What was the total of their ages 5 years ago?
   (A) 65 (B) 75
   (C) 45 (D) 55

5. A rose flower always has ____________.
   (A) Soil (B) Thorns
   (C) Petals (D) Shine

6. Observe the given image and find the figure from the following which satisfies the same relation between the shape as of the dot shown in the given figure.

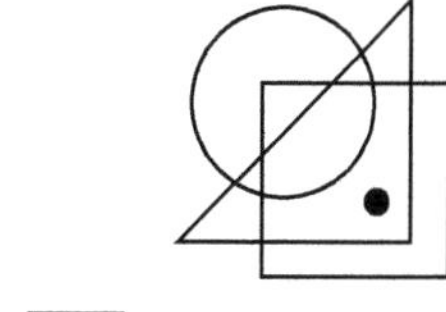

(A)  (B) 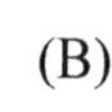

(C) 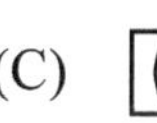  (D) 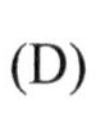 

7. Identify the figure which can replace question mark in the given figure.

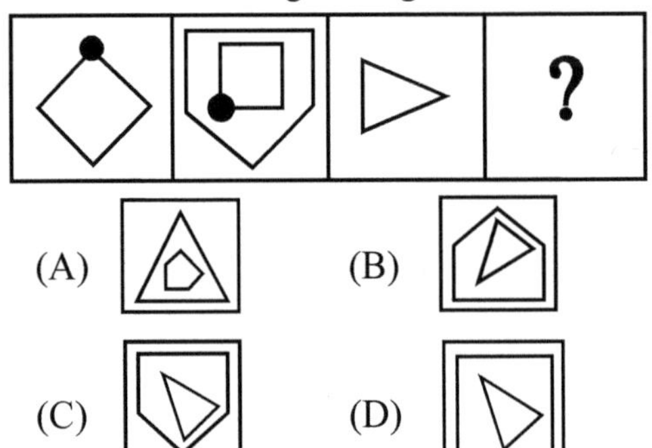

8. Identify the water image.

RAJ589D8

(A) ꓤ∀1288D8
(B) ꓭ∀1288D8
(C) ꓤ∀ſ288D8
(D) ꓭ∀ſ288D8

9. Identify the set of the series which follows the following rule.

Open figure gets closed and closed figures open up.

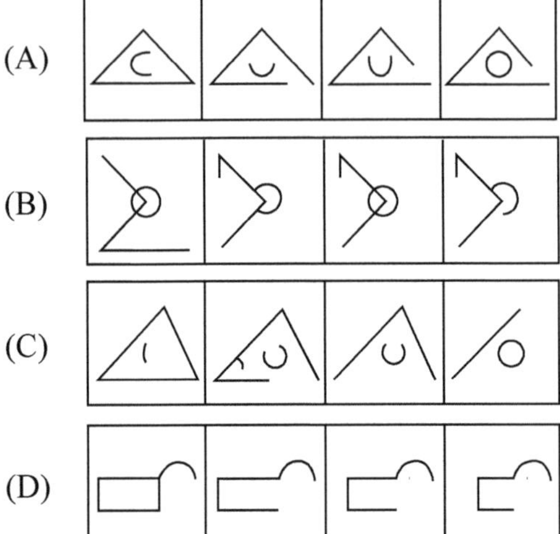

10. Count the number of triangles.

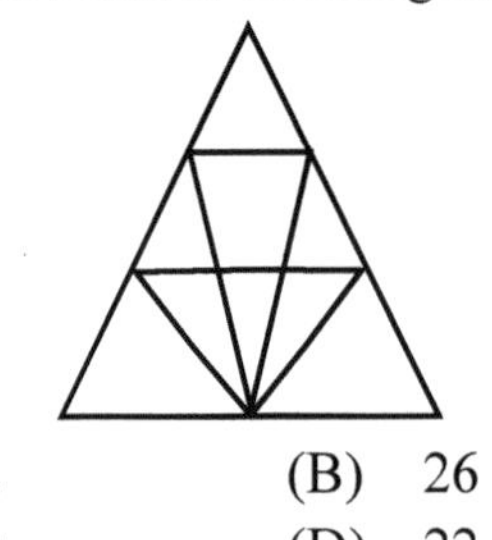

(A) 12 (B) 26
(C) 18 (D) 22

SCIENCE

11. Where does the image form when an object is placed at the centre of curvatures of a concave mirror?
   (A) Centre of curvature
   (B) Between centre of curvature and focus
   (C) Infinity
   (D) Focus

12. When an object is shifted slightly closer to a converging lens, what happens with the image?
   (A) It will decrease in size and appear moving away from the lens.
   (B) It will increase in size and appear moving close from the lens
   (C) It will decrease in size and appear moving close to the lens
   (D) It will increase in size and appear moving away from the lens

13. Carefully read the following statements and identify the correct option.
   S1: When a light ray enters into the water from air, it will bend.
   S2: When light ray enters into water from air, its speed increases.
   (A) S1 is true but S2 is false
   (B) S2 is true but S1 is false
   (C) S1 and S2 are true
   (D) S1 and S2 are false

14. Which of the following alloys is used for the formation of fuse wire?
(A) Nickle- Tungsten
(B) Tungsten-Tin
(C) Copper-Tin
(D) Tin-Lead

15. When current is passed through a conductor some heat is produced, the produced heat depends upon ______________.
(A) The time utilized for the flow of current.
(B) The material used for the formation of conductor.
(C) The impulse of current flowing through the conductor
(D) All of these

16. Identify the circuit which will allow the glowing of a bulb.
(A) 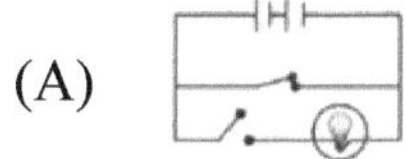
(B) 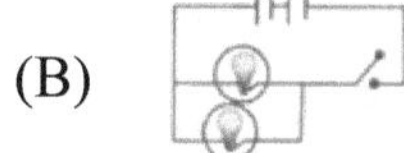
(C) 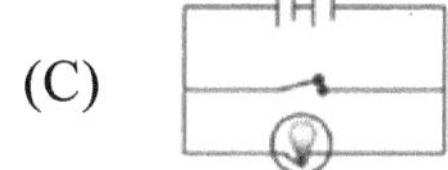
(D) 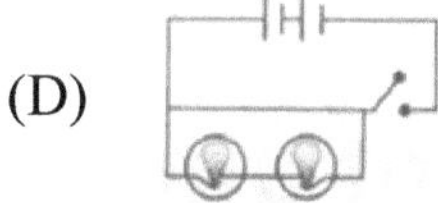

17. A train starts from a station S at 7:00 AM and reaches its destination D at 12: 00 midnight. The speed of train is 100 km/h. Calculate the distance between S and D.
(A) 1700 km (B) 1800 km
(C) 1600 km (D) 1500 km

18. Identify the correct statement regarding a moving body travelling with a constant speed along a straight path.
(A) Due to straight path the body will not change its direction.
(B) Its acceleration is zero.
(C) The velocity will change with the change in the direction of the winds.
(D) None of these

19. It is a displacement-time graph. A and B are two moving bodies that are moving with constant velocity. Mark the correct statement regarding the graph.

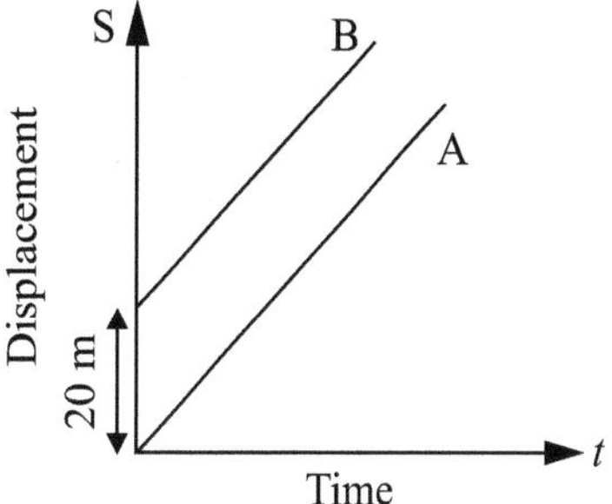

(A) A will always be 20 m behind of B.
(B) A will cover 20 m in some time.
(C) A is moving slower than B.
(D) B is moving slower than A.

20. Identify the common feature between water and wind pollinated plant species.
(A) Both the plants do not produce nectar.
(B) Both the plants produce ribbon like and long flowers.
(C) Both (A) and (B)
(D) None of these

21. Riya took two plants P1 and P2. P1 has large, coloured and nectar producing flowers while P2 has small and dull flowers which do not produce nectar. P1 has sticky and bigger pollen grains while the P2 has small and dry pollen grains. Identify the correct statement regarding P1 and P2.
(A) P1 could be pollinated by insects while P2 could be pollinated by animals.
(B) P1 could be pollinated by the animals while P2 could be pollinated by water.
(C) P1 could be pollinated by the insects while P2 could be pollinated by wind.
(D) Given information is insufficient.

22. Identify the incorrect match.
   (A) Uricotelic- Arthropods, reptiles, birds
   (B) Ammoniotelic- Protozoans, cnidarians, poriferans
   (C) Ureotelic- Mammals, adult amphibians, boy fish
   (D) None of these

23. In the bell jar experiment, a well watered plant is taken and it is covered with a bell shaped glass body. After some time, some droplets of water are seen on the inner walls of the jar. What does this experiment demonstrate?

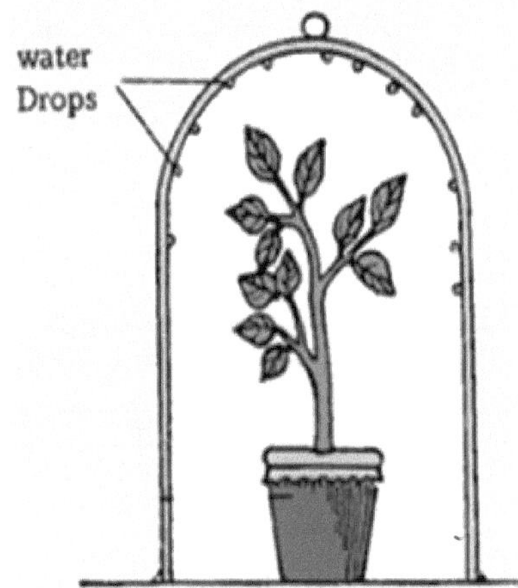

   (A) In the absence of oxygen plants starts losing water.
   (B) In the absence of surrounding carbon dioxide, the plants lose the capacity of photosynthesis.
   (C) The living nature of the plants, in the scarcity of oxygen plants try to obtain oxygen from the water.
   (D) Water droplets are formed because of the transpiration through the leaves of plant.

24. This is the image of ________ and it performs the transportation of_________.

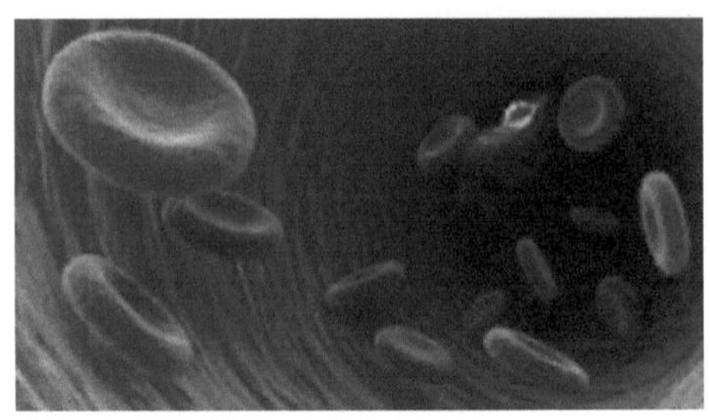

   (A) Platelets, hemoglobin
   (B) Neutrophils, antibodies
   (C) Red blood cells, oxygen
   (D) White blood cells, antibodies

25. You must have seen aquariums at many places. If a person adds warm water in the aquarium, the fish of the aquarium die. What is the reason behind it?
   (A) The gills of the fish stop working due to change in the temperature of the water.
   (B) The concentration of oxygen reduces in warm water which makes it scarce for respiration.
   (C) Fish are not adapted to tolerate the fluctuation in the temperature of the water.
   (D) All of these

26. Which of the following gases is present in higher amount in the exhaled air than in the inhaled air?
   (A) Oxygen
   (B) Carbon dioxide
   (C) Nitrogen
   (D) All of these

27. Identify the correct path of oxygen in the process of inhalation.
   (A) Trachea → Bronchi → Bronchiole → Alveoli → Nostrils → Nasal cavity → Pharynx
   (B) Nostrils → Nasal cavity → Pharynx → Trachea → Bronchi → Bronchiole → Alveoli
   (C) Nostrils → Nasal cavity → Pharynx → Bronchiole → Alveoli → Trachea → Bronchi
   (D) There is no certain path.

28. Imagine you have a pond in your garden in which you have grown many types of aquatic plants. In the breeding season of mosquitoes what should be your prime action to prevent the breeding?
 (A) You will add some goldfish into the pond.
 (B) You will spray a thin layer of oil on the surface of the water.
 (C) You will spray mosquito repellent spray on the surface of the water daily.
 (D) All of these

29. Major part of the Earth is water even then there is shortage of water in many parts of the world. Mark the correct region of shortage.
 (A) Water pollution has reduced the amount of water from the Earth.
 (B) 90% water of the Earth is frozen.
 (C) Most of the water around the Earth is not available in the usable form.
 (D) The rainwater cannot be used for drinking purpose.

30. The given flow chart shows the flow of energy in a food chain. Mark the correct statement with respect to P, Q, R and S.

Energy source → *P* → *Q* → *R* → *S*

 (A) S are scavengers which feed upon the decaying matter and clean the environment.
 (B) Q comes in action when the primary producers P die.
 (C) R are the carnivores and feed upon the other animals. R sometimes get their food indirectly from P.
 (D) Only A and C.

31. The prime factor which work on the formation of cyclones is/are ___________.
 (A) Wind Speed
 (B) Humidity
 (C) Temperature
 (D) All of these

32. Mark the correct statement.
 (A) The flow of air occurs from region of high temperature to low temperature.
 (B) The flow of air occurs from the high-pressure region to low pressure region.
 (C) The flow of air occurs from the low-pressure region to high pressure region.
 (D) The flow of air occurs from region of low temperature to high temperature.

33. A weak zone underneath the Earth is present, which causes earthquake due to sliding of plates, that zone is called as _________.
 (A) Sliding zone
 (B) Fault zone
 (C) Eruption zone
 (D) Explosive zone

34. Identify true statement(s) regarding climate.
 (A) As we move from the higher level towards the lower (sea) level, the temperature is generally higher.
 (B) In North-East India maximum rainfall occurs, therefore the climate is wet.
 (C) Both of these
 (D) None of these

35. A list of some adaptations of animals is given below. Group them according to the adaptation for polar region and rainfall region.

a: Subcutaneous fat
b: Small sized ear
c: Beautiful coloured feathers
d: Thick fur
e: Large ears
f: Sticky pads on feet
g: Long beak
h: Long tail

	Polar Region	**Rainfall Region**
(A)	a, b, c, d	e, f, g, h
(B)	c, e, f, g, h	a, b, d
(C)	a, d, f, g	b, c, e, h
(D)	a, b, d	c, e, f, g, h

36. Magnesium ribbon is burnt and obtained ash is dissolved in water, a solution S is obtained. What would be the nature of solution S when it is tested with the indicator?
   (A) It is basic solution and it will turn red litmus into blue.
   (B) It is acidic solution and it will turn blue litmus into red.
   (C) It is basic solution and it will not change the colour of indicator.
   (D) Cannot be predicted.

37. Observe the following statements and identify the type of change occurring there.
   a: Drawing the gold into gold leaf
   b: Heating of the iron piece till red hot
   c: Breaking of a glass.
   d: Inflating a balloon.
   (A) All are chemical changes
   (B) All are physical changes
   (C) a, b is chemical change
   (D) c, d is physical change

38. Litmus papers are used to distinguish the acid and bases. When treated with ____ red litmus paper turns into ___ and on treating with ____ blue litmus paper turns into ____.
   (A) Acid, red, Base, blue
   (B) Acid, blue, Base red
   (C) Base, blue, Acid, red
   (D) Base, red, Acid blue

39. Find out the example which satisfies neutralization process.
   (A) Spread of lime fertilizers in the fields to treat the acidic soil.
   (B) Use of baking powder to treat bee stings.
   (C) Brushing your teeth with the toothpaste.
   (D) All of these

40. Observe the image and mark the statement why the silver coating is done in the flask?

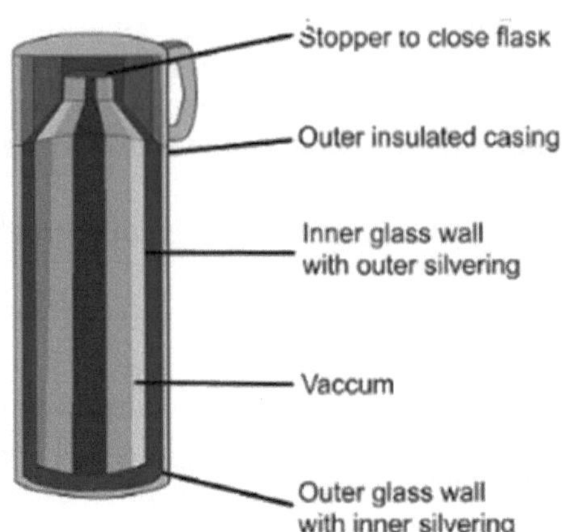

   (A) It prevents the breaking of the glass vessels due to jerk.
   (B) It reduces the flow of the heat.
   (C) It increases the convectional temperature.
   (D) It reflects the heat and reduces reflection.

41. Four types of different boxes (Iron, wood, glass and plastic) were kept in the Sun for half an hour, which box will be the hottest after a particular time?
   (A) Wood (B) Iron
   (C) Plastic (D) Glass

42. Identify the true statements regarding sericulture.
   (A) Sericulture is linked to the silk production.
   (B) By the process of reeling, silk fibers are obtained from the cocoons.
   (C) If during culture an adult comes out of the cocoon, it becomes useless for the silk production.
   (D) All are true.

43. The wool sorters sometimes get infected by bacteria ____ which causes a fatal disease to them known as _______.
   (A) Escherichia coli, wooler's disease.
   (B) Vibrio anthracis, sorter's disease.
   (C) Bascillus anthracis, sorter's disease.
   (D) None of these

44. Identify the correct sequence of digestive process.

a: Absorption of the water and salts from the undigested food.

b: Liquification of the food; initiation of protein breakdown.

c: Moistening of the food; initiation of starch breakdown.

d: Complete breakdown of proteins, carbohydrate and fats; absorption of nutrients in the blood mainstream.

(A) a, b, c, d (B) c, b, d, a

(C) b, d, a. c (D) d, a, c, b

45. A lot of nitrogen is required by most of the crops, which help them for the synthesis of the proteins. A nitrogen fixing bacterium class Rhizobium helps the plant to get nitrogen. Mark the incorrect statement regarding Rhizobium.

(A) Rhizobiumare found in the root nodules of the leguminous plants.

(B) Leguminous plants support the nutrition and shelter of the Rhizobium.

(C) These bacteria make nitrogen available for the plants by fixing atmospheric nitrogen.

(D) Rhizobium is an autotrophic class of-bacteria.

ACHIEVERS SECTION

46. Suppose, there is only one light source in your room but there are two mirrors, one convex, another concave. Which mirror will be used to make the room lighted?

(A) Either of the convex or concave, depends on the position of the light source.

(B) Only concave because it converges the light rays

(C) Only convex because it will diverge the light rays

(D) The room will remain dark because of the absence of proper lighting.

47. Four electromagnets were arranged in different manners. Identify the strongest electromagnet among all

(A)

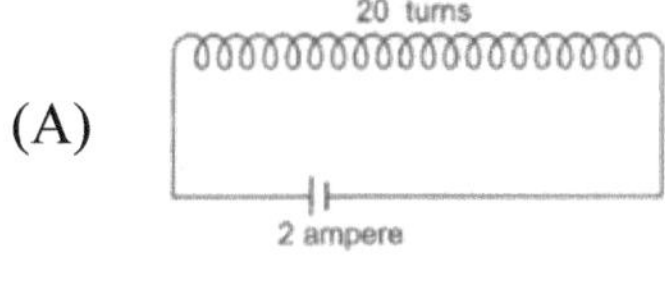

(B)

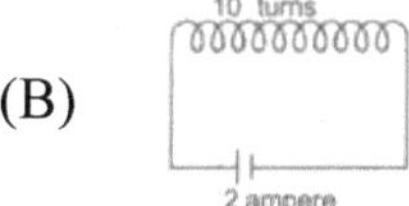

(C)

(D)

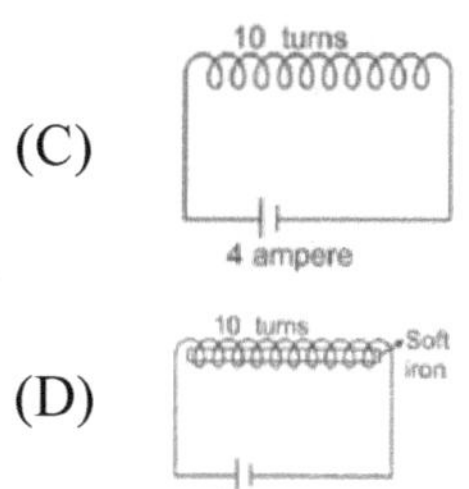

48. Carefully observe the given flow chart and mark the places which match with the characteristics of the xylem and phloem.

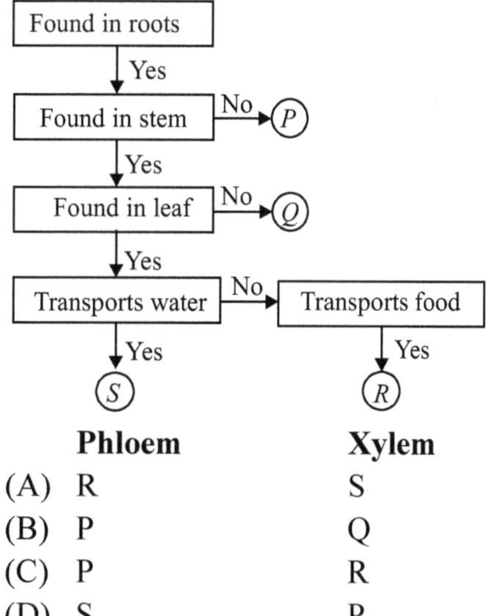

	Phloem	Xylem
(A)	R	S
(B)	P	Q
(C)	P	R
(D)	S	P

49. Three plants of same species were taken, and some investigations were performed over them. Carefully observe them.

P1: A paper bag was tied around the buds and the anthers were left untouched.

P2: Buds were tightly bound by the paper bag after careful removal of the anthers.

P3: Buds were left open to the air after removal of the anthers.

Only P3 produced seeds while others were opened normally, what can be concluded by this?

(A) Self pollination was observed in this plant species.

(B) Wind pollination was observed in that plant species.

(C) Cross pollination was observed in this plant species.

(D) No pollination was observed in that plant species.

50. Given graph depicts about the change in the volume of lungs during the breathing process. What is the meaning of change from Q to R?

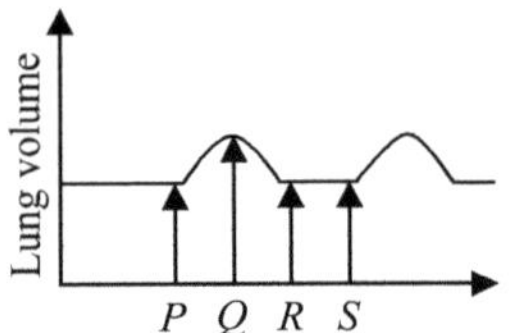

(A) Movement of air from bronchiole to lungs.

(B) Movement of air out of the lungs.

(C) Synchrony between the inhalation and heartbeat.

(D) Expansion of lung capacity.

Mock Test Paper 2

N S O

NATIONAL SCIENCE OLYMPIAD

Total Questions : 50 Time : 1 Hour

PATTERN AND MARKING SCHEME			
Section	**(1) Logical Reasoning**	**(2) Science**	**(3) Achievers Section**
No. of Questions	10	35	5
Marks per Questions	1	1	3

SYLLABUS

Section – 1: Verbal and Non-Verbal Reasoning.

Section – 2: Heat, Motion and Time, Electric Current and its Effects, Winds, Storms and Cyclones, Light, Acids, Bases and Salts, Physical and Chemical Changes, Weather, Climate and Adaptations of Animals to Climate, Fibre to Fabric, Nutrition in Plants and Animals, Respiration in Organisms, Transportation in Plants and Animals, Reproduction in Plants, Natural Resources and Their Conservation (Soil, Water: A Precious Resource, Forests our Lifeline, Wastewater Story).

Section – 3: Higher Order Thinking Questions – Syllabus as per Section – 2.

LOGICAL REASONING

1. Find out which of the following images is best suited to continue the given series.

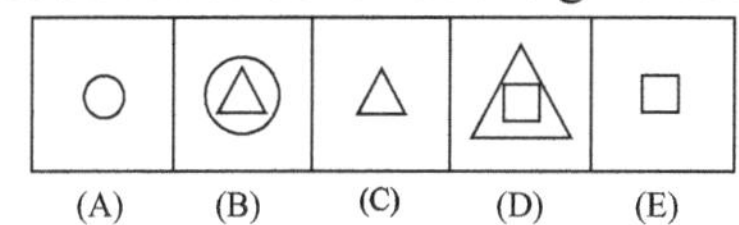

(A) (B) (C) (D) (E)

(A) (B)

(C) (D)

2. Find the odd one out.

(A) (B)

(C) (D)

3. Find out the mirror image of the given images.

Nu56p7uR

(A) ЯuƬq8ƨuИ (B) ЯuƬd9ƨuИ

(C) ЯnƬq8ƨnИ (D) Иuƨ8qƬuЯ

4. Identify the image which will resemble to the unfolded Z.

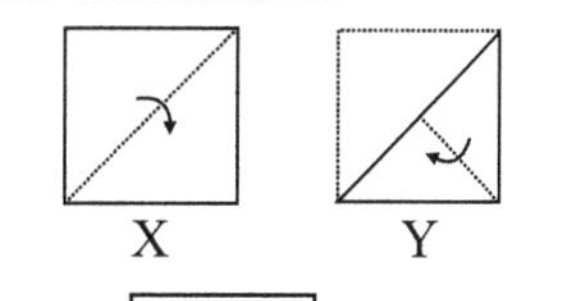

X Y Z

(A) (B)

(C) (D)

5. Using one image once, group the given figures accordingly.

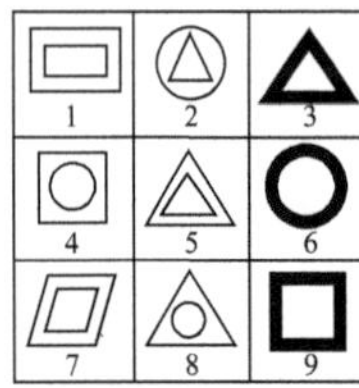

(A) 2,5,8; 1,4,7; 3,6,9
(B) 3,9,8; 1,5,7; 2,4,6
(C) 3,6,9 ;2,4,8;1,5,7
(D) 2,5,8 ;1,4,7; 3,6,9

6. Manika pointed towards Anil and said. "I am the only daughter of one of the sons of his father." What is Anil to Manika?
(A) Brother (B) Uncle
(C) Grand father (D) Cousin

7. A set of few words is given as follows. Arrange them in a meaningful sequence.
a: Hand b: Chest
c: Stomach d: Face
e: Skull f: Heel
g: Shoulder h: Thigh
i: Neck j: Knee
(A) a, b, c, h, j, f, e, d, i, g
(B) f, e, d, i, g, a, b, c, h, j
(C) i, g, a, b, f, e, d, c, h, j
(D) e, d, i, g, a, b, c, h, j, f

8. 8 kids are sitting round in a circle, facing the centre. Pavitra is second to the right of Tej who is the neighbour of Ravi and Varnika. Simran is not the neighbour of Pavitra. Varnika is adjacent to Uma. Qutub is not sitting between Simran and Whity and Whity is not sitting between Uma and Simran.
Find out two kids who are not sitting adjacent to each other.
(A) Whity and Simran
(B) Qutub and Pavitra
(C) Ravi and Varnika
(D) Cannot be determined

9. Below, two statements are given, S1 and S2. Read the statements carefully and identify the correct option regarding the sentences.
S1: Chandra Shekhar Azad, Bhagat Singh were very brave freedom fighters of our country. They fought for the freedom of our nation.
S2: The Britishers were very afraid of all the patriots and freedom fighters of our country, so they decided to leave India and declared our nation Independent in the year of 1947.
(A) S1 and S2 are independent effects.
(B) S1 is the cause and S2 is the effect of S1.
(C) S1 and S2 has no relation with respect to each other.
(D) Both statements are wrong.

10. Which of the following Venn diagrams correctly depicts the relation between Singer, Lawyer and Author?

(A)  
(B) 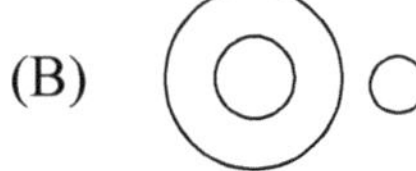
(C) 
(D) 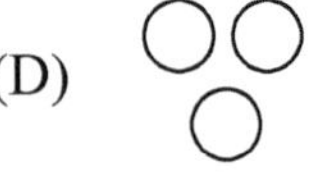

SCIENCE

11. What kind of nutrition is shown by the fungus present on the bread piece.
(A) Autotrophic nutrition
(B) Symbiotic nutrition
(C) Parasitic nutrition
(D) Saprotrophic nutrition.

12. When you eat baked potatoes, some enzymes act on processing of digestion of the potatoes starting from the mouth. Identify the sequence of the enzymes starting from the mouth towards alimentary canal.
(A) Salivary maltase → Pancreatic amylase → Trypsin
(B) Salivary amylase → Pancreatic amylase → Disaccharidase

(C) Pancreatic amylase → Salivary amylase → Lipase

(D) Salivary maltase → Lipase → Trypsinogen

13. Identify the incorrect statement.

(A) Asbestos is the only naturally obtaining mineral fibre.

(B) Hair of the sheep, which are used for the production of wool trap a lot of air.

(C) Fibroin holds the two strands of sericin of a silk fibre together.

(D) None of these.

14. Identify the false statements.

(A) Cashmere sheep is used for the production of extremely soft wool Cashmere wool.

(B) Silk is a naturally obtaining cellulosic fibre.

(C) Both (A) and (B) are false

(D) None of these

15. When a liquid is boiled, it gets converted into gas, which parameter of the substance increases?

(A) Kinetic energy

(B) Potential energy

(C) The size of the molecule

(D) All of these

16. Identify the wrong statement.

(A) During winter days black fabric is used to absorb the heat.

(B) To save ice from melting, jute sacks are used to cover the ice blocks.

(C) The thermometer bulb is held to see the reading.

(D) None of these

17. Read the following two statements and mark the correct option.

S1: The taste of acid is bitter while bases taste sour.

S2: The taste of baking soda is not sour.

(A) S1 is true and S2 is false

(B) S1 is false and S2 is true

(C) Both A and B are true

(D) Both A and B are false

18. There are two farmers F1 and F2. F1 found that the soil of his farm is basic, and F2 uses chemical fertilizers to improve the productivity. What are they suggested to add to improve the quality of the soil of their respective fields?

(A) F1: Organic matter; F2: Quick lime

(B) F1: Quick lime; F2: Organic matter

(C) F1 and F2 should use organic matter in their respective farms

(D) F1 and F2 should use some basic compounds in their respective farms.

19. Identify X and Y to complete the following reaction.

Acetic acid + Sodium hydrogen carbonate →
Sodium acetate + water + X

$X + Ca(OH)_2 \rightarrow Y + Water$

	X	Y
(A)	$CaCO_3$	CO_2
(B)	CO_2	$CaCO_3$
(C)	H_2O	CO_2
(D)	H_2O	$CaCO_3$

20. Fill in the blanks with the appropriate choices.

Dissolution of sugar in water is an example of __W__ change. If the sugar is heated in the test tube over the Bunsen's burner flame, first melting occurs, it turns into brown colour and finally turns into ___X___. The newly synthesized substance is ___Y___ and the change is known as ___Z___.

	W	X	Y	Z
(A)	Irreversible	Brown	Coal	Physical
(B)	Reversible	Brown	Coal	Chemical
(C)	Irreversible	Black	Charcoal	Physical
(D)	Reversible	Black	Charcoal	Chemical

21. Identify the behavioural adaptation.
   (A) Grey whales migrate from cold Arctic ocean to the warm water off the coast of Mexico.
   (B) Opossum are adapted to roll onto their back and slow down their breathing and become stiff to pretend as dead.
   (C) A hognose snake can act as dead to deceive their predators.
   (D) All of these

22. Identify the incorrect statement related to the animals given in the image.

   (A) Polar bear and penguins have a very strong smelling power
   (B) Polar bear has thick layer of fat under their skin and fur while penguins have a thick layer of fat beneath their skin.
   (C) Polar bear and penguins both create a large group to keep themselves warm and this also help them to easily hunt for their food.
   (D) Polar bears and penguins are good swimmer as they possess webbed feet and streamlined body.

23. Mark the correct statement.
   (A) The cyclones cannot hit the coastal regions of India because it does not produce the cyclone causing factors.
   (B) The cyclones are generated due to very high pressure and very high speed of wind and the winds revolve along with the water.
   (C) In the winter season the wind flow is from terrestrial region to coastal region.
   (D) All are correct.

24. If the Earth was not rotating on its axis, what were the consequences?
   (A) The path of air would have been straight from high pressure region to low pressure region and after equilibrium the air would have died and stopped blowing.
   (B) The path of air would have been straight from low pressure region to high pressure region and after equilibrium the air would have been died and stop blowing.
   (C) Total absence of air on the Earth.
   (D) None of these.

25. Tornadoes can be defined as ____________.
   (A) A violent and impulsive frame of air column which extends from the thunder storms up to the ground.
   (B) The wind blowing with the speed of 200 mph.
   (C) Tornadoes are the heavy thunderstorm which destructs the air balance.
   (D) None of these

26. Read the statements and mark the correct option.
   S1: Forest conservation results into the prevention of soil erosion.
   S2: The canopy at the top of the trees reduces the speed and force of the rain fall.
   (A) S1 and S2 are correct and S2 is the correct explanation of S1.
   (B) S1 and S2 are correct but S2 is not the correct explanation of S1.
   (C) S1 is true but S2 is false
   (D) S1 and S2 are false.

27. Fill in the blanks.

Top part of the tree above the trunk is known as the __X__. In the rainforests, some vegetations grow under the canopy, it is called as the ___Y___.

	X	Y
(A)	Understory	Crown
(B)	Crown	Understory
(C)	Canopy	Forest floor
(D)	None of these	

28. Identify the true statement(s).
   (A) Autotrophs are the base of a food chain.
   (B) Microbes act upon the dead organic matter to degrade them.
   (C) Both statements are true
   (D) None of the above.

29. Identify the true statement(s).
   (A) Bronchitis is the state of inflammation of bronchi which is triggered by the inhalation of polluted air.
   (B) Yeasts are anaerobically respiring organisms therefore used in the wine and beer production.
   (C) Sneezing causes the forced expulsion of the foreign particles which entered with the inhaled air.
   (D) All of these.

30. Match the column I with column II for the type of respiration

Column I	Column II
(I) Fish	a. Bronchial Respiration
(II) Insects	b. Cutaneous respiration
(III) Mammals	c. Tracheal respiration
(IV) Amphibians	d. Gills

	I	II	III	IV
(A)	d	c	a	b
(B)	a	b	c	d
(C)	b	d	c	a
(D)	d	c	b	a

31. Fill in the blanks with appropriate words.

__X__ are present in the chest cavity and the chest cavity remain surrounded by __Y__. ___Z___ may be explained as the large muscular sheet which makes the floor of the chest activity.

	X	Y	Z
(A)	Ribs	Lungs	Diaphragm
(B)	Diaphragm	Lungs	Ribs
(C)	Lungs	Ribs	Diaphragm
(D)	Bronchiole	Tracheas	Ribs

32. The correct order of formation and passage of urine is ___________.
   (A) Ureter → Bladder → Kidney → Urethra
   (B) Kidney → Ureter → Bladder → Urethra
   (C) Bladder → Kidney → Urethra → Ureter
   (D) None of these

33. The plant vessels which are used for the transportation of food are known as ___X__. The loss of water from the leaves is called as __Y__.

	X	Y
(A)	Xylem	Photosynthesis
(B)	Phloem	Transportation
(C)	Xylem	Water release
(D)	Phloem	Transpiration

34. Transportation refers to the transport of ions and other molecules from one part to another part of the body. Heart is the machine which purifies blood and blood transports many ions to different part of the body. Which part(s) of the heart carries the oxygenated blood?
   (A) Aorta and left ventricle
   (B) Aorta and right ventricle
   (C) Pulmonary artery and right auricle
   (D) Pulmonary artery and left auricle.

35. Read the following statements carefully and arrange them in a proper order with respect to maturation of the plants.

a: The shoot grows
b: It starts growing downwards due to gravitational force.
c: Development of the roots.
d: The seedlings obtain required food from the cotyledons.
e: With the growth of the plants more leaves develop.
f: The seed leaves are not required anymore, wither and fall off.
g: Development of seedling leaves to make their own food.

(A) $d \rightarrow g \rightarrow f \rightarrow e \rightarrow c \rightarrow b \rightarrow a$
(B) $e \rightarrow c \rightarrow b \rightarrow d \rightarrow g \rightarrow a \rightarrow e \rightarrow f$
(C) $c \rightarrow b \rightarrow a \rightarrow d \rightarrow g \rightarrow f \rightarrow e$
(D) Cannot be determined

36. Carefully read the following statement and identify whether these are True (T) or False (F).

a: Pollination is followed by fertilization.
b: Ripening of ovary produces seeds and ripening of ovule forms fruits after the fertilization process.
c: Natural vegetation propagation includes cutting, layering, grafting and tissue culture.
d: The seeds which are dispersed through water generally adapt the floating ability in the form of fibrous or spongy outer coat same as of coconut.

	a	b	c	d
(A)	T	F	T	F
(B)	F	T	F	T
(C)	T	T	F	F
(D)	F	F	T	T

37. Calculate the acceleration of a car attaining a speed of 40 ms^{-1} in 10 sec.

(A) 4 ms^{-2} (B) 2 ms^{-2}
(C) 10 ms^{-2} (D) 20 ms^{-2}

38. A simple pendulum, which is 3 m long and the mass of the bob is 3 kg, is oscillating. Its time period ____________.

(A) Will decrease
(B) Will increase
(C) Will be constant
(D) First increases then decreases

39. Mark the correct example of uniform motion.

(A) An airplane flying at the speed of 450 km/h towards east.
(B) A train moving with 60 km/h and reaching station.
(C) A car in the traffic.
(D) None of these

40. In which of the following appliances an electromagnet is not used?

(A) Electric heater
(B) Electric bell
(C) Washing machine
(D) Refrigerator

41. When current passes through the coil, if we increase the strength of current, flow is increased in the coil, then which of the following can be stated as true?

(A) Strength of the magnetic fields will remain unaffected.
(B) Strength of the magnetic field will fluctuate
(C) Strength of the magnetic field will decrease.
(D) Strength of the magnetic field will increase.

42. If you observe the cartons of bulbs, you will see 60 W 220 V written on it. What does it signify?

(A) Current of 220 V is flowing in the bulb and 60 W is consumed.
(B) The bulb releases 60 J energy per second, and it is connected to 220 Volt.
(C) The bulb consumes 60 J energy per second, and it is connected to 220 Volt.
(D) None of these

43. Lateral inversion property is shown by which mirror from the following?

(A) Convex mirror
(B) Concave mirror
(C) Bifocal mirror
(D) Plane mirror

44. When sunlight falls on the water droplets,

a beautiful rainbow appears. Which physical phenomena is responsible for this incidence?

(A) Dispersion, total internal reflection and refraction.

(B) Diffusion, dispersion and refraction.

(C) Only dispersion

(D) Only reflection

45. When a ray of light is incident on a concave mirror, what should be the angle of incidence from its centre of curvature?

(A) 0° (B) 45°

(C) 60° (D) 90°

ACHIEVERS SECTION

46. Observe the given food web and determine what will be the effect on this food web if the population of Buzzard is increased?

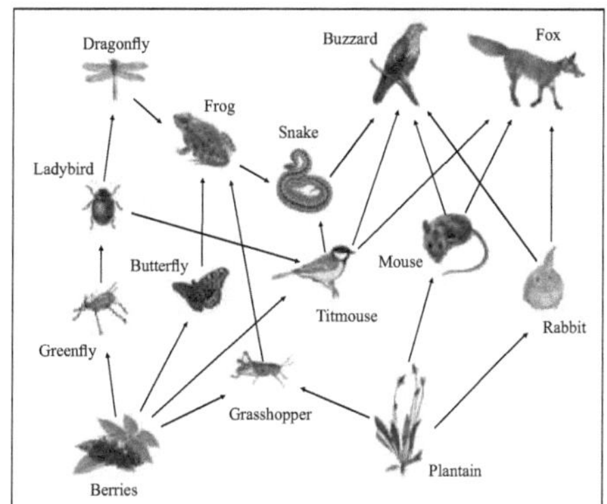

(A) The population of snake will also increase.

(B) The population of the frogs will decrease.

(C) The population of the plantain will increase.

(D) The population of the rabbit will remain unaffected.

47. Observe the glasses and suppose one balloon was tied on the mouth of each glass rod, then determine the balloon belonging to which type of water will get inflate?

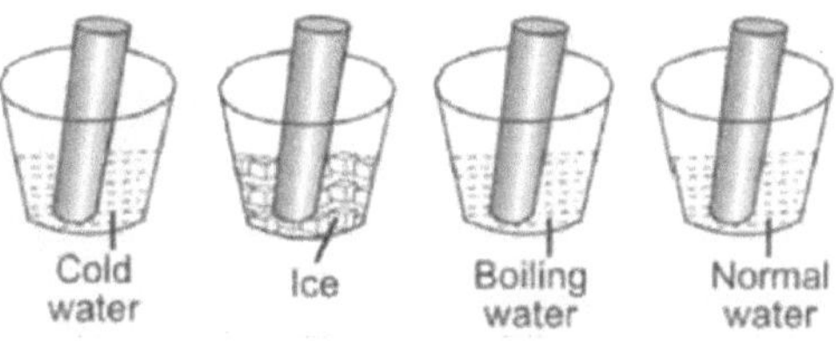

(A) Cold water (B) Ice

(C) Boiling water (D) Normal water

48. Fill in the blanks.

a: ___ glands are not found in the camel's skin.

b: Migration of the Siberian cranes from Russia to India occurs in the season of ___.

(A) Salivary, Springs

(B) Sweat, Winters

(C) Salivary, Winters

(D) Sweat, Summers

49. Mark the correct statements.

(A) Organic acids are generally weak acid, and these are used as food supplements.

(B) Inorganic acids are extremely corrosive.

(C) Both (A) and (B)

(D) None of these

50. You were given two thermometers let's say T1 and T2. Both the thermometers are showing same temperature but in different degrees, T1 in degree Celsius and T2 in degree Fahrenheit. Identify the correct option regarding the temperature.

(A) T1 has greater temperature than T2.

(B) T1 has lower temperature than T2.

(C) T1 and T2 have same temperature irrespective of their units.

(D) Cannot be determined.

NATIONAL CYBER OLYMPIAD (NCO)

Mock Test Paper 1

N C O

NATIONAL CYBER OLYMPIAD

Total Questions : 50 Time : 1 Hour

PATTERN AND MARKING SCHEME			
Section	**(1) Logical Reasoning**	**(2) Computer and IT**	**(3) Achievers Section**
No. of Questions	10	35	5
Marks per Questions	1	1	3

SYLLABUS

Section – 1: Verbal and Non-Verbal Reasoning.

Section – 2: Fundamentals of Computer, Evolution of Computers, Memory & Storage Devices, Using Windows 7, MS Word (Links, Mail Merge, Macros, Exploring Styles group), MS PowerPoint (Working with Slides Master and Themes, Advancing Slides using Hyperlink and Actions, Customizing and Broadcasting Slide Shows), MS Excel (Components of MS Excel Window, Editing and Formatting cells in a Worksheet, Introduction to Formulas, Sorting and Filtering Data, Macros, Features of Insert and Page Layout tabs), Programming in QBasic, Internet & Viruses, Networking, Latest Developments in the field of IT.

Section – 3: Higher Order Thinking Questions – Syllabus as per Section – 2.

LOGICAL REASONING

1. Maya ranked 13th from the top and 28th from the bottom in a class. How many students are there in the class?
   (A) 48 (B) 56
   (C) 40 (D) None of the above

2. Complete the analogy.
   AG : HN : : FL : ?
   (A) MS (B) YT
   (C) DH (D) RQ

3. If L stands for +, M stands for −, N stands for ×, P stands for ÷, then find the value of 14 N 10 L 42 P 2 M 8.
   (A) 280 (B) 164
   (C) 153 (D) 234

4. Identify the pattern and insert the missing digit.

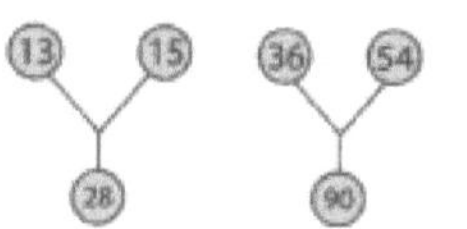

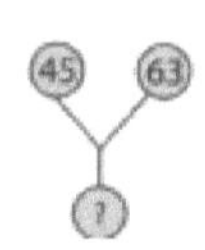

   (A) 74 (B) 59
   (C) 80 (D) 108

5. Select a figure from the options in which the figure (X) is exactly embedded as one of its part.

Fig. (X)

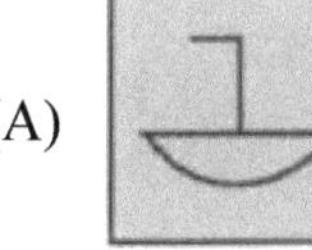
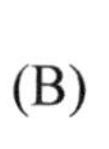
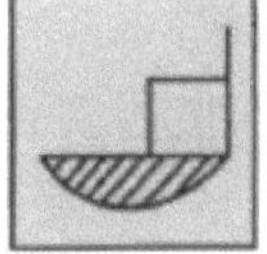
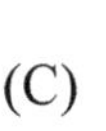
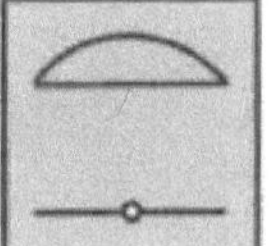

(A) (B) (C) (D)

6. Choose the correct figure from the four options which represents the sheet X after folding it along the dotted line.

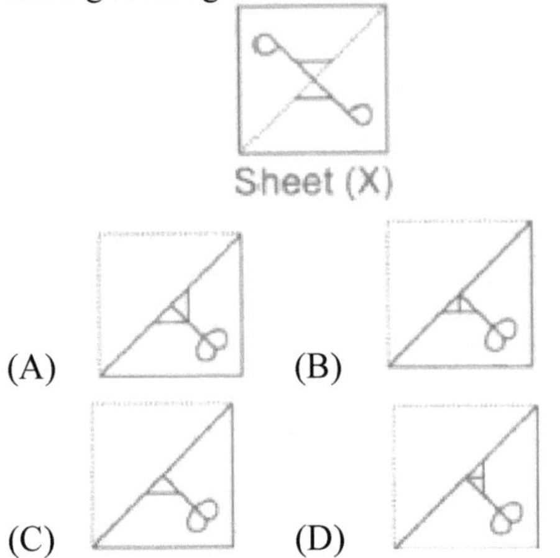

(A) (B) (C) (D)

7. Which of the following diagrams indicates the best relation between Women, Mothers and Doctors ?

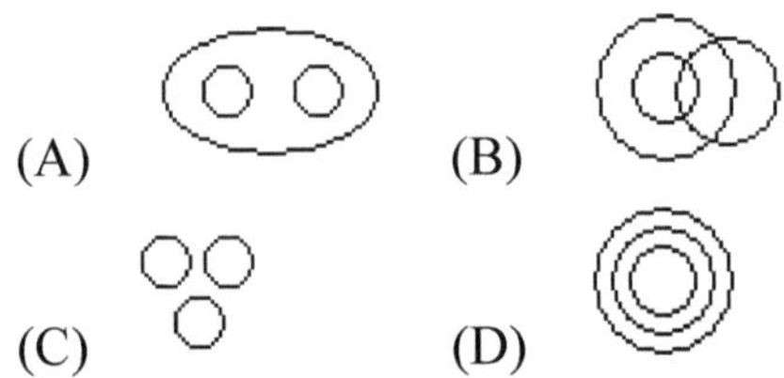

(A) (B) (C) (D)

8. In a certain code language, the word LATEST is written as IDQHPW. How will the word PAPERS be written in that language?

(A) SXSBUP (B) MDMHOV
(C) MDSBUP (D) MDMHUV

9. Choose correct mirror image of the given figure.

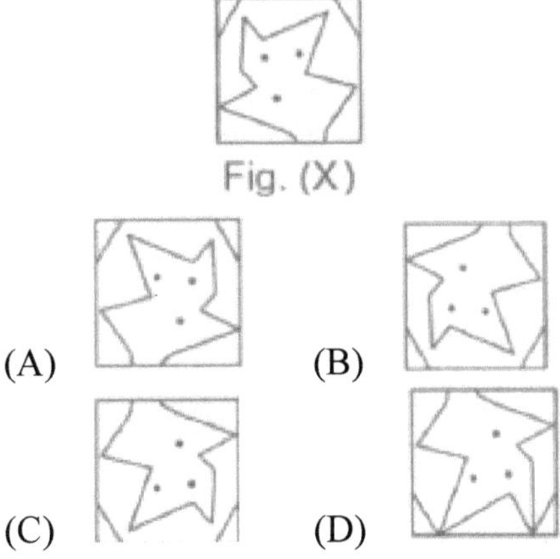

(A) (B) (C) (D)

10. How many squares are there in the given figure?

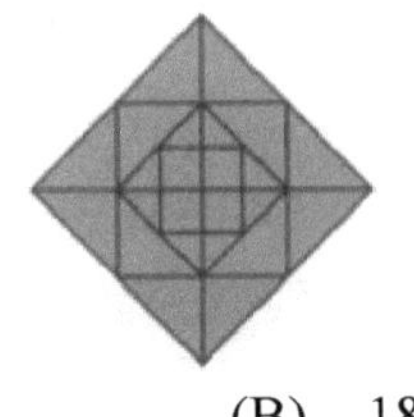

(A) 21 (B) 18
(C) 12 (D) 16

COMPUTERS AND IT

11. Identify the merge option.

(A) Merge and Center
(B) Unmerged Cells
(C) Merge Cells
(D) None of these

12. Which of the following options allows you to change desktop background, screensaver and taskbar and windows border color?

(A) Action Center (B) Personalization
(C) Snipping Tool (D) None of these

13. What is the function of Merge and Center option in MS Excel?

(A) It is used to merge the content of multiple cells into one and align it to center.
(B) It is used for wrapping text by displaying it on multiple lines.
(C) It is used for adding text effects to a cell.
(D) None of these

14. Which of the following is a series of commands and instructions used for repetitive tasks to save time while performing those tasks?

(A) Automation (B) Print Layout
(C) Macros (D) Watermark

15. _______ is a feature in Windows 7 that allows to share files and printer among connected computers.

(A) Location aware (B) Homegroup
(C) Aero Peek (D) None of these

16. ______ is the keyboard shortcut to increase the font size of the text in MS Word.
(A) Ctrl + Shift + >
(B) Alt + Tab
(C) Alt + F4
(D) Ctrl + Alt + S

17. ______ is a physical location where people may obtain Internet access, typically using Wi-Fi technology, via a wireless local area network.
(A) Hotspots (B) Wi-Fi Venue
(C) Virtual Venue (D) None of these

18. Select the correct match in context with MS Excel.
(A) - Format Cells
(B) - Insert Cells
(C) - Delete Cells
(D) - Conditional Formatting

19. 'Wrap text' icon in MS Excel is used to ______.
(A) Rotate text to a diagonal angle
(B) It is used for wrapping text by displaying it on multiple lines.
(C) Highlight interesting cells
(D) None of the above

20. Which of the following output devices converts text information into spoken sentences?
(A) Voice Response System
(B) Speech Synthesizer
(C) Voice Reproduction System
(D) None of these

21. An ____ cell refers to a cell in Excel that is currently selected.
(A) Formula cell (B) Passive cell
(C) Active cell (D) None of the above

22. Identify the following:
It forms characters and images by spraying small drops of ink on paper.
It is commonly used in homes for everyday printing.
(A) MacBook
(B) Floppy disk
(C) Inkjet printer
(D) None of the above

23. Choose the correct one for an online storage service?

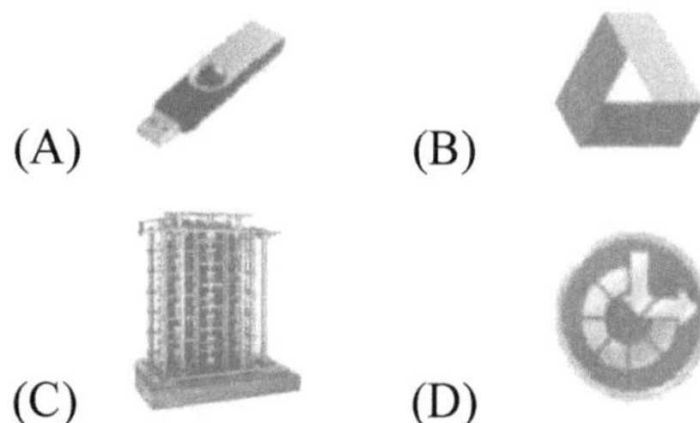

(A) (B)
(C) (D)

24. Differential equations are solved by using wheel and disc mechanisms, in case of?
(A) Differential Analyser
(B) ENIAC
(C) Ball-and-disc integrator
(D) None of the above

25. _______ is used for labelling narrow columns.
(A) Cell styles
(B) Conditional Formatting
(C) Orientation option
(D) None of these

26. _______ is first single chip microprocessor.
(A) Motorola 6800 (B) Intel 4004
(C) TMS 1000 (D) All of the above

27. Hallmark of fourth generation computers is known as?
(A) Transistor
(B) Supercomputer
(C) Artificial Intelligence
(D) Microprocessor

28. Homegroup is a home network feature in Windows 7 that allow:
(A) to share files and printer among connected computers
(B) to change the colour of your window borders
(C) to change the colour of start menu
(D) to change the color of taskbar

29. Select the odd one out.

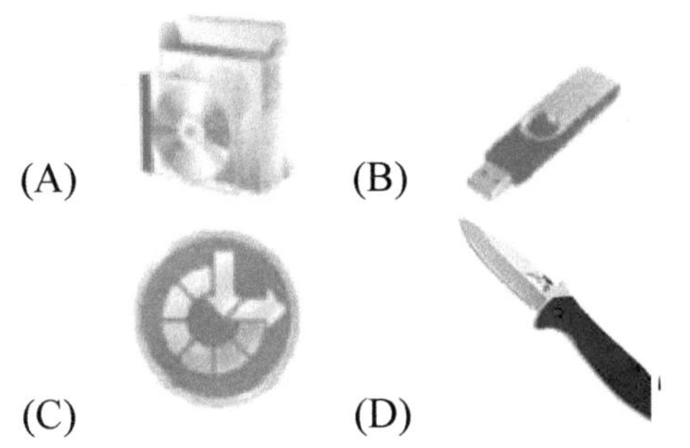

(A) (B)

(C) (D)

30. _______ is a new Windows 7 feature that helps you keep track of all of the external devices installed on your computer.

(A) Device Stage (B) Personalization

(C) E-mail (D) Device Name

31. _______ is a feature of Windows 7 to jump to parent folders or subfolders in the path of the current folder.

(A) Jump trail (B) Action Center

(C) Update Center (D) Breadcrumb trail

32. Keyboard shortcuts can be assigned by using _______.

(A) Ribbon tabs (B) Insert

(C) Macros (D) Review

33. Which of the following keyboard shortcuts is used to undo the last actions?

(A) Alt + S

(B) Shift + S

(C) Ctrl + Z

(D) CTRL + P

34. Hyperlink can be inserted by pressing the keys_______.

(A) CTRL + K

(B) Ctrl + Z

(C) CTRL + P

(D) None of the above

35. _______ are used during slide show to point at important topics.

(A) Slide sorter

(B) Slide Master

(C) Laser pointers

(D) None of the above

36. _______ the top slide that controls all information about the theme, layout, background, color, fonts, and positioning of all slides.

(A) Slide sorter

(B) Notes Master

(C) Handout Master

(D) Slide Master

37. Which of the following statements is CORRECT about Themes?

(A) You cannot change the colours of the current theme

(B) You cannot choose the background style for the current theme

(C) You can change the effect of the current theme

(D) All of the above

38. An MS Excel formula starts with_______ sign.

(A) Equal to (B) Minus

(C) Plus (D) Division

39. Match the different options given in Column-I with their corresponding names given in Column-II.

Column I		Column II	
a.		(i)	Orientation
b.		(ii)	Wrap text
c.		(iii)	Increase Indent
d.		(iv)	Merge and Centre

(A) a-(iii), b-(iv), c-(ii), d-(i)

(B) a-(iv), b-(i), c-(ii), d-(iii)

(C) a-(ii), b-(iv), c-(i), d-(iii)

(D) a-(ii), b-(i), c-(iii), d-(iv)

40. Identify the function of the given icon.

(A) It is used for adding text effects to a cell.
(B) It is used for wrapping text by displaying it on multiple lines.
(C) It is used to rotate text diagonally or vertically.
(D) It is used to align the text to left.

41. What will be the output of the following program?

```
age = 14
DO
PRINT age
age = age + 1
LOOP WHILE age <14
```

(A) 15 (B) 13
(C) 14 (D) 16

42. Write the following expression in QBASIC.

$$A = B - \frac{P^3}{C^2 \cdot B} + Q.R + T$$

(A) $A = B - P\hat{}3/(C\hat{}2 * B) + Q * R + T$
(B) $A = B + P^2/(C * B) + Q/R - T$
(C) $B = A + P\hat{}3/(C\hat{}2 * B) + Q * R + T$
(D) $A = B + P\hat{}3/(C\hat{}2 * B) + Q * R - T$

43. What will be the output of the following QBASIC code?

```
X = 9
IF (X = 8) THEN
PRINT "You selected 8"
ELSEIF (x = 7) THEN
PRINT "You selected 7"
ELSEIF {x = 6) THEN
PRINT "You selected 6"
ELSE
PRINT "You made an invalid choice"
END IF
```

(A) You made an invalid choice
(B) You selected 8
(C) You selected 7
(D) You selected 6

44. _______ is a reference to a web resource that specifies its location on a computer network and a mechanism for retrieving it.

(A) Database (B) URL
(C) Deep web (D) Search engine

45. Find the odd one out.

(A) Machine learning
(B) Virtual reality (VR)
(C) Cognitive Technology
(D) Television

ACHIEVERS SECTION

46. Match the different units given in Column-I with their corresponding values given in Column-II.

	Column I		Column II
a.	GFLOPS	(i)	10^{24}
b.	YFLOPS	(ii)	10^{15}
c.	PFLOPS	(iii)	10^{12}
d.	TFLOPS	(iv)	10^{9}

(A) a-(iii), b-(iv), c-(ii), d-(i)
(B) a-(iv), b-(i), c-(ii), d-(iii)
(C) a-(ii), b-(iv), c-(i), d-(iii)
(D) a-(ii), b-(i), c-(iii), d-(iv)

47. Identify the following:

It is a type of semiconductor memory that uses bi-stable latching circuitry (flip-flop) to store each bit.

It is typically used for CPU cache.

(A) Dynamic RAM
(B) Video RAM
(C) Static RAM
(D) Audio RAM

48. _______ units of measure for the numerical computing performance of a computer.
(A) FLOPS
(B) MIPS
(C) Both (A) and (B)
(D) None of the above

49. _______ is a feature in Apple Inc.'s macOS and iOS operating systems for printing via a wireless LAN (Wi-Fi).
(A) Net Connect Printing
(B) Location Aware Printing
(C) Air Print
(D) All of the above

50. Identify the following:
It is being currently used to train medical students for surgery.
It is a particularly useful tool for training soldiers without putting them in harmful situation.
Widely used with computer games.
(A) VR headsets (B) Mobiles
(C) Computers (D) All of the above

Mock Test Paper 2

Total Questions : 50 Time : 1 Hour

PATTERN AND MARKING SCHEME			
Section	**(1) Logical Reasoning**	**(2) Computer and IT**	**(3) Achievers Section**
No. of Questions	10	35	5
Marks per Questions	1	1	3

SYLLABUS

Section – 1: Verbal and Non-Verbal Reasoning.

Section – 2: Fundamentals of Computer, Evolution of Computers, Memory & Storage Devices, Using Windows 7, MS Word (Links, Mail Merge, Macros, Exploring Styles group), MS PowerPoint (Working with Slides Master and Themes, Advancing Slides using Hyperlink and Actions, Customizing and Broadcasting Slide Shows), MS Excel (Components of MS Excel Window, Editing and formatting Cells in a Worksheet, Introduction to Formulas, Sorting and Filtering Data, Macros, Features of Insert and Page Layout tabs), Programming in QBasic, Internet & Viruses, Networking, Latest Developments in the field of IT.

Section – 3: Higher Order Thinking Questions – Syllabus as per Section – 2.

LOGICAL REASONING

1. In a certain code 'GOLD' is written as '5124' and 'LIVE' is written as '2983'. How is 'VOID' written in that code?
   (A) 8394 (B) 8194
   (C) 8154 (D) 8793
2. Monika is standing at point X, facing North-East. She turns 3 right angles in the anti-clockwise direction. Which direction is she facing now?
   (A) North (B) East
   (C) South-West (D) South-East
3. Select the correct water image of the figure (X) from the given alternatives.

(A)  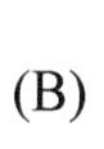 (B) 

(C) 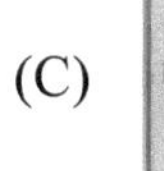  (D) 

4. Which of the following options will replace the (?) in the given series?
   8, 16, 32, 56, ?
   (A) 74 (B) 48
   (C) 88 (D) 100
5. Find one word which cannot be formed from the letters of the given word.
   WEBPAGE
   (A) WEB (B) PAGE
   (C) AGE (D) WET

6. Pointing to Abhay. Sahil said to Prerna, "The mother of his father is the wife of your maternal grandfather". How is Prerna related to Abhay ?
   (A) Niece (B) Mother
   (C) Wife (D) Cousin

7. Two positions of a dice are shown. When 4 is at the bottom, what number will be on the top?

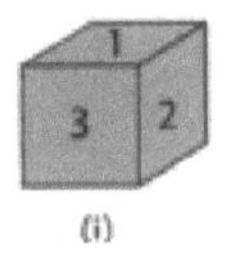
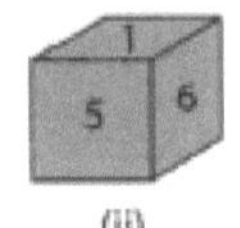

   (A) 1 (B) 2
   (C) 5 (D) 6

8. Select a figure from the options which do not satisfy the same condition of placement of the dots as in Fig. (X).

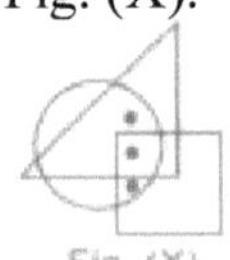

Fig. (X)

(A)   (B) 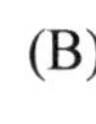

(C)  (D) 

9. Complete the figure matrix.

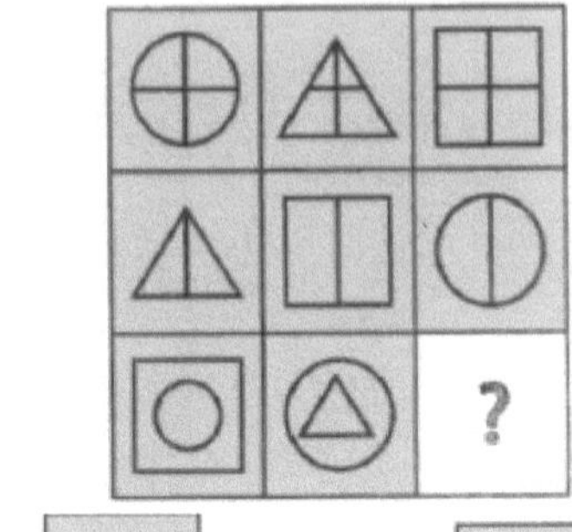

(A) 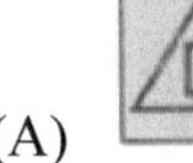  (B) 

(C) 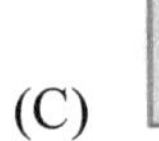 (D)  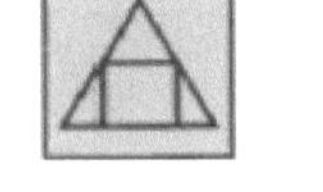

10. Select the figure from the options in which Fig. (X) is exactly embedded as one of its part.

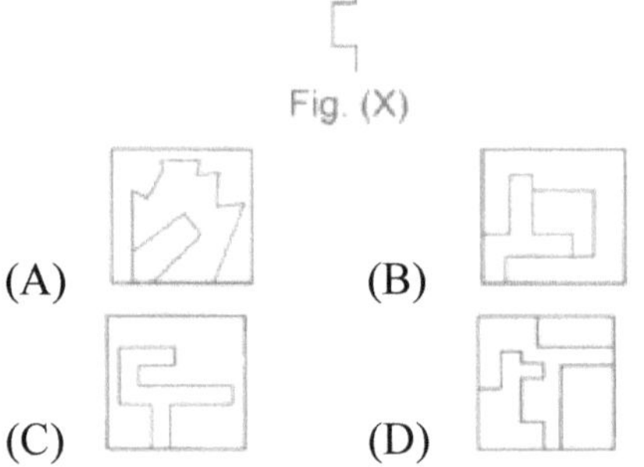

Fig. (X)

(A) (B)

(C) (D)

COMPUTERS AND IT

11. These scanners provide a flat, glass surface to hold a sheet of paper, book or object for scanning. These scanners are called _____ scanners.
    (A) Handheld (B) Drum
    (C) Flatbed (D) None of these

12. The software that acts as an interface between the user and the world wide web is ________.
    (A) Internet (B) E-mail
    (C) Web browser (D) None of these

13. Which of the following is the keyboard shortcut to select the entire row containing the current cell in MS Excel 2010?

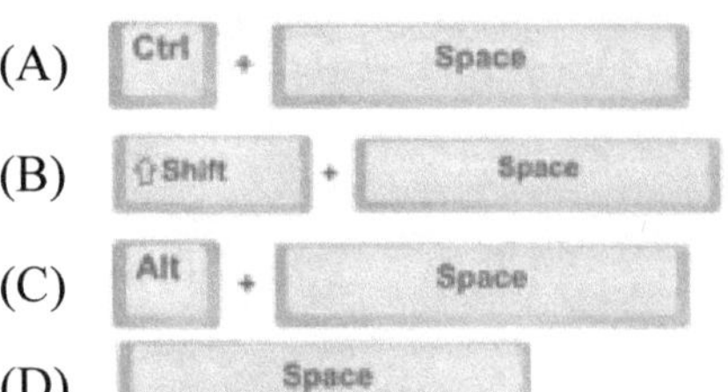

14. The smallest unit of data in a computer which has a single binary value either 0 or 1 is called _______.
    (A) Nibble (B) Bit
    (C) Byte (D) None of these

15. Which of the following is a processor?
(A) Floppy Disk (B) OMR
(C) Intel Core i7 (D) None of these

16. Which of the following is used to format cells as per the pre-defines styles?
(A) Wrap Text (B) Cells Styles
(C) Orientation (D) Editing

17. MS Excel is a _____ program.
(A) presentation (B) word processing
(C) spreadsheet (D) table sheet

18. Select the incorrect match.
(A) Voice Response System – it enables a computer to talk to a user.
(B) Search Engine - Lycos
(C) Intel 4004 – First single chip micro-processor
(D) Insert a hyperlink – Alt + K

19. _______ is a utility in windows to increase access speed by rearranging files stored on a disk to occupy contiguous storage, so that disks and drives can work more efficiently.
(A) Formatting
(B) snipping tool
(C) Disk defragmenter
(D) None of these

20. The function of the given icon is _____.

(A) It is used to rotate text diagonally or vertically.
(B) It is used to insert new cells.
(C) It displays the format cells dialog box.
(D) None of the above

21. Find the odd one out.

(A) (B)

(C) (D)

22. _______ is a robot designed for agricultural purposes.
(A) Artificial intelligence
(B) Augmented reality
(C) Agri bot
(D) None of the above

23. How many numbers of colors are used in favicon of google?
(A) 4 (B) 5
(C) 6 (D) 3

24. _______ is used for presenting laser generated 3D images of objects in a real environment.
(A) Oculus Rift (B) Oculus Go
(C) HoloLens (D) All of the above

25. _______ sends the recorded information to third parties without the user's knowledge.
(A) Pen drive (B) URL
(C) Spyware (D) Key bloggers

26. Technology which converts electrical signals carrying data to light and sends the light through transparent glass fibers about the diameter of a human hair.
(A) Fiber optic (B) DSL
(C) BPL (D) None of the above

27. _______ is a specially designed website that brings information from diverse sources, like emails, online forums and search engines, together in a uniform way.
(A) Hotspots (B) Web portal
(C) Wi-Fi (D) All of above

28. Web servers are embedded in devices such as,
(A) Printers (B) Routers
(C) Webcams (D) All of the above

29. _______ allows you to position the cursor for the next piece of text output.
(A) Locate (B) Canvas
(C) Screen (D) None of the above

30. _______ reads barcodes and converts them into electric pulses to be processed by a computer.
(A) Barcode reader (B) Light pen
(C) Optical mark reader (D) Monitor

31. Find the odd one out.
(A) Cache memory (B) RAM
(C) ROM (D) Hard disk

32. The first iPad was released in _______.
(A) 2008 (B) 2007
(C) 2006 (D) 2010

33. Match the different options given in Column-I with their corresponding names given in Column-II.

Column I		Column II	
a.		(i)	Clear all formatting
b.		(ii)	Text highlight color
c.		(iii)	Arrange the current selection in alphabetical or numerical order.
d.		(iv)	Change the color behind the selected text, paragraph or table cell.

(A) a-(iii), b-(iv), c-(ii), d-(i)
(B) a-(iv), b-(i), c-(ii), d-(iii)
(C) a-(ii), b-(iv), c-(i), d-(iii)
(D) a-(ii), b-(i), c-(iii), d-(iv)

34. _______ displays a line according to the coordinates.
(A) GOTO command
(B) LINE command
(C) Circle command
(D) None of the above

35. Write the following expression in QBASIC.

$$A = B + \frac{P^2}{C \cdot B} - Q.R + T$$

(A) $A = B - P^\wedge 2/(C^\wedge 2 * B) + Q * R + T$
(B) $A = B + P^2/(C * B) - Q/R - T$
(C) $A = B + P^2/(C * B) - Q * R + T$
(D) $A = B + P^\wedge 2/(C * B) + Q * R - T$

36. ________ is a standard network protocol used for the transfer of computer files between a client and server on a computer network.
(A) FTP (B) RAM
(C) CPU (D) File activator

37. By entering _______ in a worksheet will show current date.
(A) Ctrl + $4
(B) 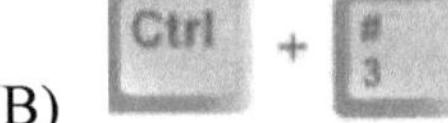

(C) Ctrl + :
(D) 

38. By pressing ______ in worksheet, one can spell check.
(A) F4 (B) 

(C) Ctrl + F7 (D) 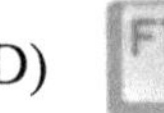

39. Which of the following icons is used to apply the same look of a content to other content in the document?
(A) (B)
(C) (D) A

40. _______ is used to edit the appearance of presentation handouts, including the layout, headers and footers, and background.
(A) Handout master
(B) Slide master
(C) Notes master
(D) None of the above

41. You can split a word document by pressing _______ keys.
(A) 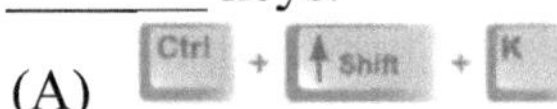

(B) Shift + H + K
(C) Ctrl + Alt + S
(D) Alt + K

42. _______ is the automated process of breaking words between lines to create more consistency across a text block.
(A) Hyphenation (B) Bookmarks
(C) Watermarks (D) All of the above

43. _______ allows you to keep information in sync between your computer and files stored

in folders on network servers.
(A) Action Center (B) Sync Center
(C) Media Center (D) Update Center

44. Floating point operations per second (FLOPS) is a measure of computer_______.
(A) Data storage (B) Performance
(C) Properties (D) None of the above

45. Identify the following:
Used for storing digital information.
Used in portable electronic devices, such as digital cameras, mobile phones, laptop computers, tablets.
(A) Memory card (B) Rom
(C) Ram (D) All of the above

ACHIEVERS SECTION

46. Match the different names given in Column-I with their corresponding units given in Column-II.

Column I		Column II	
a.	kFLOPS	(i)	yotta-FLOPS
b.	YFlops	(ii)	kiloFLOPS
c.	ZFlops	(iii)	zettaFlops
d.	MFLOPS	(iv)	mega-FLOPS

(A) a-(iii), b-(iv), c-(ii), d-(i)
(B) a-(iv), b-(i), c-(ii), d-(iii)
(C) a-(ii), b-(iv), c-(i), d-(iii)
(D) a-(ii), b-(i), c-(iii), d-(iv)

47. Identify the following:
It is the program a personal computer's microprocessor uses to get the computer system started after you turn it on.
It manages data flow between the computer's operating system and attached devices.
(A) Device driver (B) BIOS
(C) Device manager (D) Hard disk

48. Which of the following options offers web portal services? (A) Naver(B) iGoogle
(C) AOL (D) All of the above

49. Match the different options given in Column-I with their corresponding matching given in Column-II.

Column I		Column II	
a.		(i)	Select an area you would like to print.
b.	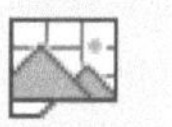	(ii)	Change page orientation
c.			Choose page size
d.		(iv)	Choose a picture for your background in worksheet.

(A) a-(iii), b-(iv), c-(ii), d-(i)
(B) a-(iv), b-(i), c-(ii), d-(iii)
(C) a-(ii), b-(iv), c-(i), d-(iii)
(D) a-(ii), b-(i), c-(iii), d-(iv)

50. Match the different options given in Column-I with their corresponding matching given in Column-II.

Column I		Column II	
a.		(i)	Set up slide show
b.		(ii)	Hide the current slide
c.		(iii)	Record from current slide
d.		(iv)	Present the slide show online

(A) a-(iii), b-(iv), c-(ii), d-(i)
(B) a-(iv), b-(i), c-(ii), d-(iii)
(C) a-(ii), b-(iv), c-(i), d-(iii)
(D) a-(ii), b-(i), c-(iii), d-(iv)

INTERNATIONAL ENGLISH OLYMPIAD (IEO)

Mock Test Paper 1

INTERNATIONAL ENGLISH OLYMPIAD

Total Questions : 50 Time : 1 Hour

PATTERN AND MARKING SCHEME				
Section	(1) Word and Structure Knowledge	(2) Reading	(3) Spoken and Written Expression	(4)Achievers
No. of Questions		45		5
Marks per Questions		1		3

SYLLABUS

Section – 1 : Spellings, Collocations and Words related to Travel, Locations, Activities, Homonyms and Homophones, etc. Synonyms, Antonyms, Analogies and Spellings, One word, Phrasal Verbs and Idioms, Modals, Word order, Nouns, Pronouns, Verbs, Adverbs, Adjectives, Articles, Prepositions, Conjunctions, Punctuation, Tenses, Voices and Narration, etc.

Section – 2 : Search for and retrieve information from various text types like News Stories, Brochures, Formal and Informal Letters and Advertisements. Understand information given in News Reports, Brochures, Itinerary, etc., Acquire broad understanding of and look for specific information in Short Narratives, Biographies, Notices and Messages etc.

Section – 3 : Ability to understand situation-based variations in functions like Requesting and Refusing, Apologies and stating of Preferences and Expression of Intent, etc

Section – 4 : Higher Order Thinking Questions - Syllabus as per Sections 1, 2 and 3.

WORD AND STRUCTURE KNOWLEDGE

1. Mark the correct spelling of the synonym of 'Important'.
   (A) predominent (B) prodominent
   (C) predominant (D) predetermined
2. Prohibit: Forbid :: Valour : ?
   (A) Courage (B) Coward
   (C) Vanity (D) Wakeup
3. Quit: Continue :: Gallant: ?
   (A) Discourteous (B) Impolite
   (C) Coward (D) All of these
4. Mark the odd one out.
   Independent, free, self- reliant, self- conscious, self- sufficient, maverick
   (A) self- conscious (B) Independent
   (C) self- sufficient (D) maverick
5. Provide one word for the following information.
   The person who travels in the spacecrafts.
   (A) Traveler (B) Astronaut
   (C) Astrologer (D) Astroscientist
6. While travelling, a group of people who are travelling together, is called as:
   (A) Convoy (B) Platoon
   (C) Caravan (D) Party
7. What is a collocation term for a person who writes about the travel experience of visiting various places?
   (A) tour guide (B) travel writer
   (C) traveler (D) journey planar

8. Identify the word which is homophonic to 'throw'

(A) Through (B) Thorough
(C) Threw (D) Throat

9. 'Hatch' is a homonym of:

(A) adjective and adverb
(B) noun and pronoun
(C) noun and preposition
(D) noun and verb

10. Complete the sentence with the suitable option.

We enjoyed the lunch party very much, ____?

(A) weren't we (B) aren't we
(C) didn't we (D) haven't we

11. Fill in the blank with suitable noun.

We don't need to rush drive, we have ___ time to reach airport.

(A) more of (B) plenty of
(C) rich of (D) matter of

12. Insert the appropriate pronoun.

Don't worry papa. Shashank will take care of ____.

(A) themselves (B) myself
(C) itself (D) himself

13. Insert the suitable adverb.

The glass vessels should be carried ____ as these are fragile.

(A) carefully (B) harshly
(C) frequently (D) lately

14. Fill in the blanks with suitable verb.

The lion is said to be the king of the jungle. The lion ____ very loudly to ___ out other animals.

(A) screams, fright (B) roars, freak
(C) trumpet, afraid (D) bark, scare

15. Fill in the blank with quantitative adjective.

Since _____ years you both are studying together?

(A) too many (B) how many
(C) how much (D) what much

16. Insert the suitable article.

____ Rabindra Nath Tagore wrote Kamayani.

(A) A (B) An
(C) The (D) None of these

17. Insert the suitable preposition.

______ Bhagwat Geeta, soul is immortal.

(A) Considering to
(B) In the place of
(C) According to
(D) It is about

18. Fill in the blank with suitable phrasal verb.

Rohit was requested to _____ while his call was being transferred to relevant person.

(A) hang up (B) hold on
(C) build up (D) make up

19. Complete the proverb.

A little knowledge is a ______ thing

(A) inevitable (B) respectful
(C) dangerous (D) proficient

20. What do you understand by the idiom 'building castle in the air'?

(A) thinking about the impractical and impossible ideas
(B) making a very beautiful building
(C) buiding a place which is beyond imagination
(D) none of these

21. Fill in the blank with the appropriate conjunction.

I worked hard to score full marks in my exam ____ I could not get full marks.

(A) so (B) but
(C) therefore (D) as

22. Complete the following sentence with all the helping verbs belong to past tenses.

When I ___ for the picnic with my family we ___ so much fun at the picnic spot. We ___ badminton and many outdoor games. It ___ a wonderful day.

(A) going, have, played, were

(B) had gone, will have, having, played

(C) was going, were having, thrown away, has been

(D) went, had, played, was

23. Complete the following sentence with correct option.

Britishers ____ over India for than 200 years.

(A) had been ruled (B) had ruled

(C) ruled (D) was ruling

24. Change the voice of the following sentence.

Anshika wrote a letter to her cousin.

(A) A letter was written by Anshika to her cousin.

(B) Her cousin was written a letter by Anshika

(C) A letter was written by Anshika for her cousin

(D) None of these

25. Identify the active voice of the following sentence.

The cows are fed by my grandfather daily.

(A) The cows are fed by my grandfather daily.

(B) My grandfather feeds the cows daily.

(C) Daily the cows are fed by my grandfather.

(D) None of these

26. Convert direct speech into indirect speech.

Vishakha said, "I love to play outdoor games, but my younger sister likes indoor games."

(A) Outdoor games are loved by Vishakaha while indoor games are liked by her younger sister.

(B) Vishakha said that she loved playing outdoor games but her younger sister liked indoor games.

(C) Vishakha and her younger sister loved outdoor games and liked indoor games.

(D) Vishkha loved outdoor games but her sister liked indoor games.

27. Identify the actual interconversion in the speech about the followings sentence.

Policeman said that he had caught the thief just then.

(A) The thief has been caught by the policeman just now.

(B) Just now the thief has been caught by the policeman.

(C) The thief would have been caught by the policeman just then.

(D) Policemen said, "I have caught the thief just now."

28. Insert the suitable modal verb in the blank.

I ____ score highest in the class this year.

(A) may (B) might

(C) should (D) ought to

29. Punctuate the followings sentence.

ramya said my father mr Ashish is a IAS officer

(A) Ramya said my father Mr Ashish is the IAS officer.

(B) Ramya said that, "my father Mr Ashish is a IAS officer."

(C) Ramya said, "My father, Mr. Ashish, is an IAS officer."

(D) none of these

30. Arrange the following words in an order to get a meaningful sentence.

punished/ he/ misbehaviour/ be/ his/ will/ for

(A) His misbehavior will punish him.

(B) His punishment will be his misbehavior

(C) He is misbehavior will be punished

(D) He will be punished for his misbehavior

Following is a notice displayed on the notice board of the school. Read it carefully and provide answers of the questions.

SABHYATA INTERNATIONAL SCHOOL NOIDA

NOTICE

09th Feb 20XX

An inter-school swimming competition has been fixed between the teams of our school and the team of Delhi International School. The competition is scheduled for the date 11th March 20XX at 9:00 AM onwards. The venue of the competition is club house swimming pool. The participants have to report at 8:00 AM in the morning and they will be taken to the venue along with their respective class teachers. Come forward and show your talent.

Sarthak

Sports Captain

31. What kind of notice is this?
   (A) Warning (B) Challenging
   (C) Volunteer (D) Informative

32. What do you understand by notice now?
   (A) Notice is a piece of information which tells about the competitions only.
   (B) The notices are displayed by the schools only.
   (C) Notices are the prior notification and information for the upcoming events.
   (D) Can't be determined.

Read the poem carefully

A simple Child:

That lightly draws its breath, and feels its life in every limb. What should it know of death?

I met a little cottage Girl:

She was eight years old, she said; Her hair was thick with many a curl that clustered round her head.

She had a rustic, woodland air and she was wildly clad:

Her eyes were fair, and very fair; Her beauty made me glad.

"Sisters and brothers, little Maid, How many may you be?"

"How many? Seven in all," she said, and wondering looked at me.

"And where are they? I pray you tell." She answered, "Seven are we;

And two of us at Conway dwell, And two are gone to sea.

"Two of us in the church-yard lie, My sister and my brother;

And, in the church-yard cottage, I Dwell near them with my mother."

"You say that two at Conway dwell, And two are gone to sea,

Yet ye are seven! I pray you tell, Sweet Maid, how this may be."

Then did the little Maid reply,

"Seven boys and girls are we; Two of us in the church-yard lie, Beneath the church-yard tree."

"You run about, my little Maid, Your limbs they are alive;

If two are in the church-yard laid, Then ye are only five."

"Their graves are green, they may be seen,"

The little Maid replied, "Twelve steps or more from my mother's door, And they are side by side.

"My stockings there I often knit, My kerchief there I hem;

And there upon the ground I sit, And sing a song to them.

"And often after sun-set, Sir,

When it is light and fair, I take my little

porringer, And eat my supper there.

"The first that died was sister Jane;

In bed she moaning lay, Till God released her of her pain; And then she went away.

"So in the church-yard she was laid;

And, when the grass was dry, Together round her grave we played, My brother John and I.

"And when the ground was white with snow, And I could run and slide,

My brother John was forced to go, And he lies by her side."

"How many are you, then," said I,

"If they two are in heaven?" Quick was the little Maid's reply, "O Master! we are seven."

"But they are dead; those two are dead! Their spirits are in heaven!"

Taws throwing words away; for still

The little Maid would have her will, And said, "Nay, we are seven!"

William Wordsworth

33. How many sisters and brothers are little maid?
    (A) seven (B) five
    (C) two (D) three

34. How many years old the little maid was?
    (A) seven (B) eight
    (C) nine (D) ten

35. Where are the four brothers and sisters of little maid?
    (A) all four at sea
    (B) all four at Conway dwell
    (C) two at Conway dwell and two at sea
    (D) two are dead and two are waiting at home

Read the following conversation carefully.

Amar: Hello! Is this Ahalya's place.

Afzal: Yes, please. May I know who is there?

Amar: I am Amar, Ahalya's classmate. Where is she?

Afzal: Sorry baby. She has gone to market with her mother. Can I take your message for her?

Amar: Oh sure. In fact, I wanted to convey her that today's tennis practice has been suspended because the coach is not well. Instead the coaching will be resumed tomorrow. So, she need not to come at the court today. Could you please pass this message to her?

Afzal: Oh! Sure. Thank you.

Amar: Thank you too!

36. What is the type of the conversation?
    (A) Informative (B) Arguing
    (C) Challenging (D) Playful

37. Why did Afzal ask, "Can I take you message?"
    (A) To convey the important message to respective person.
    (B) He wanted to know why Amar has called
    (C) He didn't want to call Ahalya for the call.
    (D) He was not aware of importance of the message.

38. Why did Amar say thank you at the end of the conversation?
    (A) To end up the call
    (B) To show his friendly nature
    (C) To show his courtesy to Afzal to convey his message.
    (D) It is a ritual.

SPOKEN AND WRITTEN EXPRESSIONS

39. Identify the correctly punctuated sentence.
    Mr. Shastri, principal of my school has been transferred to a new school in Mumbai
    (A) Mr. Shastri, principal of my school, has been transferred to a new school in Mumbai.
    (B) Mr. Shastri principal of my school; has been transferred to a new school in Mumbai.
    (C) Mr shastri! principal of my school has been transferred to a new school in Mumbai!
    (D) Mr shastri; principal of my school has been transferred, to a new school in Mumbai!

40. Mayuri will tell us about her real world experience on Saturday
   (A) mayuri will tell us about her real world experience on Saturday!
   (B) Mayuri will tell us about her real-world experience on Saturday.
   (C) mayuri; will tell us about her real world experience on Saturday!
   (D) Mayuri; will tell us about her real/ world experience on Saturday.

41. Which of the following sentence is correct according to the past perfect continuous tense?
   (A) The train departed before I could reach to the platform
   (B) The train must have been departed before I reached at platform.
   (C) I could have reached at platform, but the train had started.
   (D) The train had been started before I reached at the platform.

42. Complete the sentence with past participle.
   I ___ tired but my sister ___ still energetic. In fact, I ____ tired for three days now.
   (A) am, was, was
   (B) was, was, have been
   (C) am, am, had been
   (D) none of these

43. Mark the correct responses for the following situations.
   Auto driver: Is there anyone for sector 62?
   Passenger: _____________
   (A) Yes, we reached there
   (B) Which stop is this?
   (C) Yes, I'll get down.
   (D) You don't need to stop.

44. Your best friend: I am getting shifted to Mumbai along with my parents.
   You: _______________
   (A) Do you know anyone in Mumbai?
   (B) What will you do there?
   (C) Oh, that's really great! But I'm going to miss you.
   (D) Alas! You will miss me there.

45. Complete the following conversation.
   Chetna: Hello!
   Hema: Could I speak to Mr. Ram?
   Chetna: Papa is not home right now. _______ can I take your message?
   (A) I don't want to.
   (B) I don't want to bother.
   (C) Is it very urgent?
   (D) If it is not official.

ACHIEVERS SECTION

46. Identify the indirect speech of the following sentence.
   Nisha said, "I cannot ride a bicycle."
   (A) Nisha said that she could not ride a bicycle.
   (B) Nisha says that she is unable to ride a bicycle.
   (C) A bicycle is impossible to be ride by Nisha
   (D) Nisha says that she cannot ride a bicycle.

47. Complete the following sentence with the help of given hints.
   I __helping verb __not sure __conjunction part 1__ the cricket match will be telecasted today __conjunction part 2___not.
   (A) am, either, or
   (B) is, either, or
   (C) are, neither, nor
   (D) am, whether, or

48. Identify the suitable idiom for the following situation.
   'Harish was fighting with his five years old sister to get control over the TV remote. Their father saw them fighting and asked their mother what was going on between them. Mother replied it's _______; they are

capable for fighting throughout the day.

(A) A fun activity

(B) the last chance

(C) the tip of the iceberg

(D) grasping at straw

49. Identify the sentence with correctly arranged adjectives and adverb.

(A) In the zoo my old five years niece was terrified to see the giant black horrible wolf.

(B) My five years old niece in the zoo was terrified to see the horrible black giant wolf.

(C) My five years old niece was terrified to see the horrible giant black wolf in the zoo.

(D) To see the horrible giant black wolf my five years old niece was terrified in the zoo.

50. Identify the suitable phrasal verb to replace the underlined part.

The students ended writing their papers and <u>submit their answer sheets</u> to the invigilator and left the room.

(A) landed over the answer sheet

(B) handed in the answer sheets

(C) keenly submitted the answer sheets

(D) leave out the answer sheets

Mock Test Paper 2

Total Questions : 50 Time : 1 Hour

INTERNATIONAL ENGLISH OLYMPIAD

PATTERN AND MARKING SCHEME				
Section	(1) Word and Structure Knowledge	(2) Reading	(3) Spoken and Written Expression	(4)Achievers
No. of Questions		45		5
Marks per Questions		1		3

SYLLABUS

Section – 1 : Spellings, Collocations and Words related to Travel, Locations, Activities, Homonyms and Homophones, etc. Synonyms, Antonyms, Analogies and Spellings, One word, Phrasal Verbs and Idioms, Modals, Word order, Nouns, Pronouns, Verbs, Adverbs, Adjectives, Articles, Prepositions, Conjunctions, Punctuation, Tenses, Voices and Narration, etc.

Section – 2 : Search for and retrieve information from various text types like News Stories, Brochures, Formal and Informal Letters and Advertisements. Understand information given in News Reports, Brochures, Itinerary, etc., Acquire broad understanding of and look for specific information in Short Narratives, Biographies, Notices and Messages etc.

Section – 3 : Ability to understand situation-based variations in functions like Requesting and Refusing, Apologies and stating of Preferences and Expression of Intent, etc

Section – 4 : Higher Order Thinking Questions - Syllabus as per Sections 1, 2 and 3.

WORD AND STRUCTURE KNOWLEDGE

1. Arrange the following words in a meaningful order.
   hard/ leads/ success/ to/ always/ to/ you
   (A) Success always leads you to hard work always.
   (B) Hard work always leads you to success.
   (C) Hard work is success to you always.
   (D) None of these

2. Read the followings sentence and identify the correctly punctuated sentence.
   alas the tsunami destroyed everything in chennai.
   (A) ALAS! the Tsunami destroyed everything in Chennai.
   (B) Alas? The tsunami destroyed everything in Chennai.
   (C) Alas, the tsunami destroyed everything in Chennai.
   (D) Alas! The Tsunami destroyed everything in Chennai.

3. Fill in the blank with modal verb, with the suitable options given.
   I ____ go to market to buy thing for me, my mother does it for me.
   (A) might not (B) ought to
   (C) have to (D) need not

4. Change the narration of the following sentence.
   My younger brother said to me, "When will you buy me a new laptop?"
   (A) My younger brother asked me when I would buy him a new laptop.
   (B) My younger brother asked me to buy a new laptop for him.
   (C) When a new laptop will I buy for him, my younger brother asked to me.
   (D) None of these

5. Which of the following is the correct direct speech of the following sentence.

Biology teacher said that we inhale oxygen and exhale carbon dioxide.

(A) It was told to us by biology teacher that we inhale oxygen and exhaled carbon dioxide.

(B) Biology teacher said, "We should inhale oxygen and exhale carbon dioxide."

(C) Biology teacher said, "We inhale oxygen and exhale carbon dioxide."

(D) None of these

6. Covert the following sentence into active voice.

The water bodied have been polluted by the disposal of the garbage.

(A) The water body disposal has polluted the garbage.

(B) The disposal of the garbage has polluted the water bodies.

(C) The garbage pollution has been polluted the water bodies.

(D) The water bodies will be polluted by the garbage.

7. Change the voice of the sentence.

When will Asma purchase new books?

(A) Would new books be purchase by Asma?

(B) Asma would purchase new books.

(C) Will Asma Purchase new books?

(D) When will new books be purchased by Asma?

8. Fill in the blank with the suitable option.

When I ______ with my niece she ____ with joy.

(A) was played, were dancing

(B) were played, was bubbling

(C) was playing, was bubbling

(D) played, was dancing

9. Complete the sentence with the help of hints given in the brackets.

We __ **(present continuous)** __ shortage of electricity supply __**(preposition)**___10 days. Plenty of our important works are __**(verb)**__. So, the ward members ___ **(present tense)**__ to __**(verb)**__ an email to the authorities.

(A) were facing, the, holding, had decides, send

(B) had been facing, since, holding, wrote

(C) will have been tolerating, since, waiting, sent

(D) are facing, for, on hold, have decided, write

10. Fill in the blank with suitable conjunction.

_____ he tells me his requirements I can't help him.

(A) Unless (B) till

(C) because (D) further

11. Identify the best fitted idiom for the situation 'when a person is so kind hearted, and he does not wish to physically hurt anybody.'

(A) not hurt a fly

(B) hive of activity

(C) as keen as mustard

(D) born with silver spoon

12. What does the proverb 'barking dogs seldom bite' stands for?

(A) the dogs never bite without barking

(B) the people who say often they're going to do this actually do nothing.

(C) the bad people are bitten by barking dogs

(D) the barking dogs can threaten you without barking

13. Insert the suitable phrasal verb.

Ravi was not feeling well so her mother cooked his favorite pudding to _____.

(A) make over (B) get over

(C) cheer up (D) put up

14. Insert suitable preposition.

You should study hard ____ to score good marks in your studied.

(A) for the sake of (B) in order to

(C) accordingly (D) because

15. Insert the suitable article.

____ Madhushala is a famous poetry written by ___ Dr. Harivansh Rai Bacchan

(A) the, a
(B) the, the
(C) a, the
(D) no article, no article

16. Identify the odd set of adjectives.

(A) Wooden, plastic, silk
(B) tiny, huge, giant
(C) circular, oval, rectangular
(D) gorgeous, black, new

17. Insert the suitable verb.

The Moon ___ around the earth and the Earth ___ the Sun

(A) circulate, circulate
(B) wanders, wanders
(C) collapse, collapse
(D) revolves, revolves

18. Fill in the blank with suitable adverb.

Jack is a British, but he can speak Hindi ______

(A) frankly (B) frequently
(C) fluently (D) normally

19. Insert the suitable reciprocal pronoun.

Teamworking makes us learn about working for _______.

(A) everyone
(B) each and everyone
(C) one another
(D) each other

20. Provide abstract noun for the following:

Leaves and raindrops

(A) whistle and buzz
(B) Lub dub and screech
(C) rustle and patter
(D) hum and rumble

21. Arrange the following parts of sentence in a meaningful sequence with the help of codes provide.

a: India is the second most populated country of the Asia.

b: India is the third largest country of Asia.

c: Asia is the largest continent of the world.

d: Russia is the largest country of Asia.

(A) a, b, c, d (B) c, d, b, a
(C) d, c, b, a (D) a, c, b, d

22. Identify the set of meaning of homonym 'evening'.

(A) a time between day and night and a name
(B) a time between day and night and commenting on the person
(C) a time between day and night and the time to take snacks
(D) a time between day and night and a point near to the end.

23. Mark the correct set of homophones.

(A) advice, advise
(B) advance, educate
(C) hair, ear
(D) nose, rose

24. Which type of activity is 'hiking'?

(A) fun (B) competition
(C) adventure (D) entertaining

25. An activity which is exciting and daring, is called as:

(A) Adventure (B) Travel
(C) Entertainment (D) Amusement

26. Give one word for the following information.

The properties which provide protection from the disease causing microbes.

(A) Analgesic (B) Antiseptic
(C) Antibacterial (D) Antifungal

27. Mark the odd one out.

Infection, allergy, disorder, injury, syndrome.

(A) Infection (B) disorder

(C) syndrome (D) injury

28. Deny : Affirm :: Condemn: ?

(A) Acquit (B) start

(C) attack (D) affirm

29. Fiction : Imaginary :: ? : Hardworking

(A) Intelligent (B) Diligent

(C) Wisdom (D) Courage

30. Mark the correct spelling of the place which is very low in pressure.

(A) Vaccum (B) Vacuum

(C) Vacume (D) Vaccuume

READING

Following a small paragraph taken from the biography of Dr. A.P.J. Abdul Kalam. Read it carefully and answer the questions that follows.

"His hopes of becoming a fighter pilot was dashed when he narrowly missed out on a spot with the Indian Air Force. Kalam instead joined the Defence Research and Development Organization (DRDO) as a senior scientific assistant in 1958. After moving to the newly formed Indian Space Research Organization (ISRO) in 1969, he was named project director of the SLV-III, the first satellite launch vehicle designed and produced on Indian soil.

Returning to the DRDO as director in 1982, Kalam implemented the Integrated Guided Missile Development Program. He then became the senior scientific adviser to India's defence minister in 1992, a position he used to campaign for the development of nuclear tests.

Kalam was a key figure in the May 1998 Pokhran-II tests, in which five nuclear devices were detonated in the Rajasthan Desert. Although the tests resulted in condemnation and economic sanctions from other world powers, Kalam was hailed as a national hero for his staunch defence of the country's security."

31. What do you understand by 'his hopes of becoming a fighter pilot was dashed'?

(A) He fulfilled his hopes

(B) He had more than required hopes

(C) His hopes were destroyed.

(D) He was not capable in fulfilling his own hopes.

32. Identify the correct description of the underlined words.

(A) The person who gives advices in the scientific fields.

(B) A scientist who gives advices in any field.

(C) A person who belong to advisory committee of scientists

(D) none of these

33. Identify the true difference between biography and autobiography.

(A) Autobiography are the modern version of biography.

(B) Biographies are written by the person himself while autobiography are written by others.

(C) Biographies are hand written while autobiographies are published on the social media.

(D) Autobiography are the life stories written by self and biography are the life stories written by other person.

An example of informal letter is as follows. Read them carefully and answer the connecting questions.

Room No. 201

International Hostel

Ghaziabad

12th Feb 20XX

Dear Sister,

Please accept my heartiest wishes on your forthcoming birthday. This is for the very first time in our life when I'm not with you to celebrate your birthday. I sincerely wish you achieve more and more success in your chosen desired path in your career.

Well, tell me how do you plan to celebrate your birthday? Will you go outing with your friends. <u>I wish I could come to you, but my board exams are coming so I won't be able to take liberty from my studies.</u> I have bought a small gift for you which is your favourite thing. I hope you'll like it.

Hope to see you soon.

With lots of love and wishes.

Yours affectionately,

Sarthak

34. What do you understand by the type of letter whether the sister is elder to the writer or younger to him?
    (A) She is elder to the writer
    (B) She is younger to the writer
    (C) She is twin of writer
    (D) Can't be determined.

35. What is the meaning of the underlined sentence?
    (A) He is not free to study.
    (B) He doesn't want to miss his studies
    (C) He doesn't want to attend the celebration.
    (D) None of these

The following lines belong to the biography of Rabindra Nath Tagore.

"Let us not pray to be sheltered from dangers but to be fearless when facing them." said once, one of the most heroic poets of India, at a time when the country was going through a tumultuous period during the British rule. Rabindranath Tagore, one of the epoch-making figures of the twentieth century, is one of the most widely acclaimed wordsmiths of India. Often hailed as Gurudev or the poet of poets, Tagore, through the sheer brilliance of his narratives and incommensurable poetic flair, laid an ineffaceable impression on the minds of his readers. A child prodigy, Tagore, showed a penchant for literature, art and music from a very young age and in due course of time, produced an extraordinary body of work which changed the face of Indian literature. However, he was not just a mere poet or writer; he was the harbinger of an era of literature which elevated him to the stature of the cultural ambassador of India. Even today, decades after his death, this saint-like man, lives through his works in the hearts of the people of Bengal who are forever indebted to him for enriching their heritage. He was the most admired Indian writer who introduced India's rich cultural heritage to the West and was the first non-European to be bestowed the prestigious Nobel Prize.

36. What is the title given to Rabindranath Tagore?
    (A) Acharya (B) Netaji
    (C) Gurudev (D) Leader

37. Which prize did he win?
    (A) Nobel Prize
    (B) Oscar Award
    (C) Best Poet Award
    (D) None of these

38. Provide the best suited answer in the following situation.

    Your friend went for a music concert last night. Even after the availability of the tickets you rejected to go with him. Now he explained about the concert and now you regret why didn't you go. What would be your possible answer?
    (A) Thank god! I didn't come with you. I'd gone mad.
    (B) Why didn't you tell me earlier that you are going to have fun?
    (C) Did you really enjoy?
    (D) I wish I'd gone with you.

39. Dinesh: Can you please tell me when the bus for Agra will depart?

    Receptionist: ________________
    (A) I don't know, ask the bus driver.
    (B) Bus driver will better tell you about it, I don't know.
    (C) One moment, please let me check.
    (D) I'll tell you later, buy the ticket first.

40. You are a speaker at the school annual function. How will you start your welcome speech?
    (A) I knew it already that you all will come to attend the annual function of our school because your respective kids are participants.
    (B) Thanks for coming at the function, you may collect snacks from the counter.
    (C) I'd like to welcome you all at the annual function of our school. It's a pleasure to have you here.
    (D) I am feeling very proud to see you all here.

41. Identify the correctly punctuated sentence.
    (A) Hurray, we're going on the School Picnic.
    (B) Hurray! We're going on the school picnic.
    (C) Hurray; we're going on the School Picnic!
    (D) Hurray; "we're going on the School Picnic."

42. Grandmother said to me finish your homework and sit near me. Identify the correctly punctuated sentence.
    (A) Grandmother said to me, "Finish your homework and sit near me."
    (B) grandmother said to me to finish your homework and sit near me
    (C) "Grandmother said to me finish your homework and sit near me"
    (D) Grandmother; said to me, finish your homework and sit near me!

43. Identify the correct passive voice.
    (A) The thief and the guard ran away.
    (B) The thief ran away because of the guard.
    (C) The guard ran away the thief
    (D) The thief was made to run away by the guard.

44. Complete the sentence according to the tense present tenses.

    Siya and Kanha ____ siblings. They___ in a big house. Their father ___ a prestigious businessman.
    (A) are, reside, is (B) is, gone, was
    (C) are, lived, was (D) none of these

45. Complete the sentence according to the present perfect continuous negative tense.

    They ____ living there so they don't know the actual situation of that place.
    (A) hadn't been (B) haven't been
    (C) hasn't been (D) aren't been

46. Change the voice of the following sentence.

The carpenter will have made the table by tomorrow.

(A) the table would be made by the carpenter.

(B) the table would been made by the carpenter by tomorrow.

(C) the carpenter would have been made the table by tomorrow.

(D) The table would have been made by the carpenter by tomorrow.

47. Complete the following sentence with the hints given in the bracket.

The streets (past continuous) full of water because it (past perfect continuous) continuously since past 10 hours.

(A) had, was raining

(B) was, were raining

(C) did, have rained

(D) were, had been raining

48. Insert the suitable participle preposition.

He was ____the behaviour of his classmate so he decided to talk _____ his behaviour.

(A) annoying to, according

(B) crying at, about

(C) frustrated with, regarding

(D) none of these

49. Arrange the following parts of the sentence in a meaningful sentence.

I: as I love being

II: I like to visit

III: between the mountains

IV: Himachal Pradesh again and again

(A) IV, III, II, I

(B) II, IV, I, III

(C) III, I, II, IV

(D) cannot be determined

50. Provide one word for 'the onset of puberty and development of a child into an adult.'

(A) Adolescence (B) Condolence

(C) Curriculum (D) Adulthood

Hints and Solutions

INTERNATIONAL MATHEMATICS OLYMPIAD (IMO)

MOCK TEST PAPER – 1

ANSWERS									
1. (B)	2. (B)	3. (D)	4. (B)	5. (C)	6. (C)	7. (A)	8. (A)	9. (C)	10. (B)
11. (A)	12. (C)	13. (C)	14. (A)	15. (A)	16. (D)	17. (B)	18. (B)	19. (B)	20. (A)
21. (C)	22. (C)	23. (B)	24. (A)	25. (C)	26. (C)	27. (C)	28. (D)	29. (A)	30. (B)
31. (A)	32. (B)	33. (D)	34. (C)	35. (A)	36. (B)	37. (C)	38. (C)	39. (D)	40. (C)
41. (B)	42. (D)	43. (A)	44. (B)	45. (B)	46. (A)	47. (A)	48. (A)	49. (D)	50. (B)

1. (B) Right half of the shape is deleted.

2. (B) Brother of my wife — My brother-in-law; Son of Kanika's brother is the brother-in-law of Ashish. So, Kanika's brother is Ashish's father-in-law i.e., Kanika is the sister of Ashish's father-in-law.

3. (D) As per the given code, the alphabets are coded as follows: A C C E P T is coded as 455978.

4. (B)

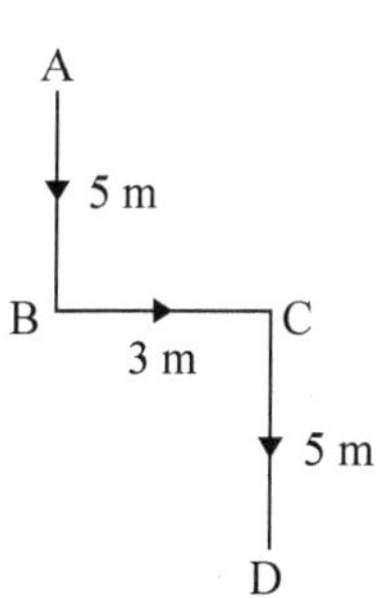

Hence, Vihaan will face towards South in the end.

5. (C) We obtain the following letter series on reversing the order of the alphabets.
Z Y X W V U T S R Q P O N M L K J I H G F E D C B A
Required letter is (14 – 12) = 2nd letter from your left in the arrangement.

6. (C) 28Z7P8T6Y4
$28 \div 7 \times 8 - 6 + 4 = 4 \times 8 - 6 + 4 = 32 + 4 - 6 = 30$

7. (A)

$$= \sqrt{12^2 + 5^2}$$

8. (A) Unfolded form of Z

9. (C) No. of cubes in the given figure is 10.

10. (B) In each column, the 3rd figure is obtained by vertically inverting the upper part of 1st figure.

12. (C) Water image

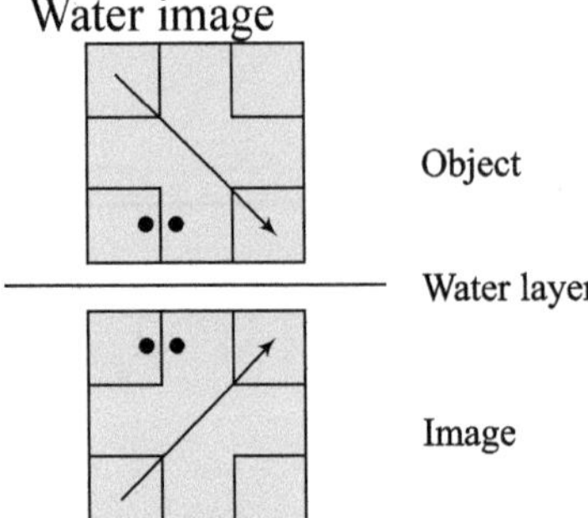

13. (C) Minimum number of straight lines is 9.

14. (A) As it has four shaded parts out of total, other figures have three shaded parts.

15. (A) Here the pattern is (3 × 2 – 1) = 5, (8 × 4 – 1) = 31, (9 × 3 – 1) = 26

16. (D) We have

$$\frac{(16a^2)^{\frac{1}{2}} \times (36a^4)^{\frac{-1}{2}}}{2a^{\frac{1}{2}} \times 5a^{\frac{3}{2}} \times 8a^{\frac{9}{4}}} = \frac{(2)^{4\times1/2} a \times 6^{-1} a^{-2}}{80a^{1/2+3/2+9/4}}$$

$$= \frac{(2)^2 \times 6^{-1}}{80a^{1/2+3/2+9/4+2-1}} = \frac{1}{120a^{21/4}}$$

17. (B) Let original fraction be $x/x + 3$;
According to question:
$x + 2/ x + 5 = = 2/3; 3x + 6$
$= 2x + 10; x = 4$
Numerator is 4, Denominator is
4 + 3 = 7
Hence, original fraction is 4/7

18. (B) ∠RQT = 60° + 60° = 120° [Exterior angle = sum of interior opposite angles]

19. (B) Place value is 3/10

20. (A) $\frac{7}{8} - \left(-\frac{11}{4}\right) + x = 3\frac{7}{24}$

7/8 + 11/4 + x = 79/24
x = –1/3

21. (C) 124 × 4 – 3 + 118 ÷ 2 = 496 – 3 + 59 = 552

22. (C) x = 120° (Linear pair)
y = 30° (As PR = RS)

23. (B) Let the no. be x
According to question
x – 4 = 80% of x
x = 20

24. (A) CP = 100/80 × 600 = ₹ 750
CP = ₹ 750, Gain = 25%
SP = 125/100 × 750 = ₹ 937.50

25. (C) No. of beakers required is
3/6 × 24 = 12

26. (C) A : B : C = 1/2 : 1/3 : 1/4 ; A : B : C = 6 : 4 : 3

27. (C) We have

$$A = P + I = P + \frac{PTR}{100}$$

$$A - P = \frac{PTR}{100}$$

$$\text{So, } \frac{A_1 - P_1}{A_2 - P_2} = \frac{P_1T_1R_1}{P_2T_2R_2}$$

$$\Rightarrow \frac{95-85}{A_2 - 102} = \frac{85 \times 3 \times R}{102 \times 5 \times R}$$

$$\Rightarrow A_2 - 102 = 20 \Rightarrow A_2 = 122$$

28. (D) We have

$$\frac{m}{5} + 8 = 4 - 3m$$

$$\frac{m+40}{5} = 4 - 3m$$

$$m + 40 = 20 - 15m$$

$$16m = -20$$

$$m = -5/4$$

29. (A) ΔABC ≅ ΔDEF is by RHS criterion.

30. (B) Part of book read in 1 hour is 1/3
Part of book read in $2\frac{1}{5}$ hours is 11/5 × 1/3 = 11/15

31. (A) $(2x - 10)° + (x - 11)° = 90°; x = 37°$

32. (B) Let sum of four numbers be y and excluded numbers be x.

Then $\frac{y+x}{5}=27$ and $\frac{y}{4}=25$

$x+y=135$ and $y=100$

$\Rightarrow x=35$

34. (C) Length of wire is $2\pi \times 42 = 84\pi$ cm
Let x be the side of the square.
$4x = 84\pi$
$x = 21\pi$
Area of circle is $\pi \times 42 \times 42$
Area of square is $21\pi \times 21\pi$
Ratio = 14 : 11

35. (A) The shape given below has exactly two flat faces.

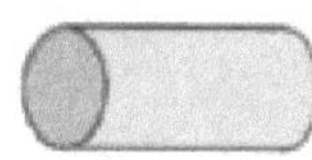

36. (B) Total fruits are 23; No. of apples is $23-p$

37. (C) Let total votes polled be x
Winning candidate got 70% votes.

So, $\frac{70x}{100}-\frac{30x}{100}=15000$

$\Rightarrow x=15000\times\frac{100}{40}=37500$

Votes polled for the winning candidate

$=\frac{70x}{100}=\frac{70}{100}\times 37500$

$=26250$

38. (C) By Pythagoras theorem,
Length of the ladder

$\sqrt{576+100}=\sqrt{676}=26$ m

39. (D) We have,

$P=\frac{45\times 100}{9\times 1}=500$

40. (C) CP = 100/80 × 13500 = ₹ 16875

41. (B) Let total pages = x

3/5 x + 80 = x
x – 3/5x = 80
2x/5 = 80
x = 400/2 = 200

42. (D) No. of pieces = 30 ÷ $3\frac{3}{4}$ = 8 pieces

43. (A) 5 km towards South

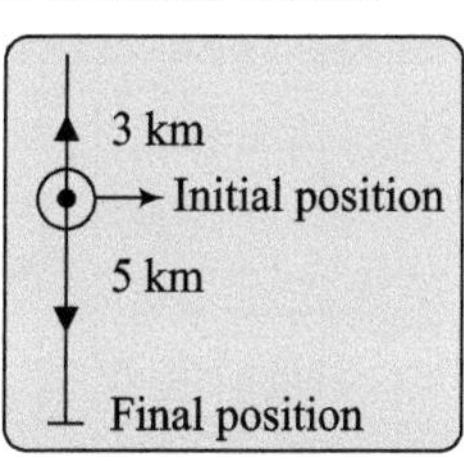

44. (B) Let the number of marbles that Shobha should give Gaurav be 'x'.
According to question

$(96+x)=2(63-x)$

$\Rightarrow 3x=30$

$\Rightarrow x=10$

45. (B) Perimeter of plot is 2(500 + 100)
= 1200 m
Cost of fencing is 1200 × 150
= ₹ 180000

46. (A) We have

$p+\frac{1}{q+\frac{1}{r}}=\frac{25}{19}=1+\frac{6}{19}$

$=1+\frac{1}{\frac{19}{6}}=1+\frac{1}{3+\frac{1}{6}}$

On comparing both sides fractions,
$p=1, q=3, r=6$

47. (A) Perimeter of the given figure is 58 cm.

48. (A) Total weight of 10 apples is 520 g
Error in weight = 10 × 10 = 100 g
Correct weight = 520 + 100 = 620 g
Average weight = 620/10 = 62 g

49. (D) Distance covered by its tip in 1 hour
= Circumference of the circle
Distance = 2 × 22/7 × 14 = 88 cm

50. (B) XW || YZ

$\Rightarrow \angle YWX = \angle ZYW = 28°$

$\Rightarrow x = 180° - (40° + 28°)$

$= 180° - 68° = 112°$

MOCK TEST PAPER – 2

ANSWERS

1. (A)	2. (D)	3. (B)	4. (C)	5. (B)	6. (A)	7. (A)	8. (A)	9. (C)	10. (C)
11. (C)	12. (C)	13. (D)	14. (C)	15. (C)	16. (C)	17. (D)	18. (B)	19. (A)	20. (A)
21. (C)	22. (C)	23. (C)	24. (B)	25. (B)	26. (D)	27. (A)	28. (A)	29. (B)	30. (D)
31. (D)	32. (C)	33. (C)	34. (D)	35. (C)	36. (C)	37. (C)	38. (B)	39. (A)	40. (D)
41. (B)	42. (A)	43. (B)	44. (C)	45. (C)	46. (C)	47. (D)	48. (B)	49. (D)	50. (B)

1. (A) In one step, a line segment is removed from one set of slanting lines and in the next step a line segment is removed from the other set of slanting lines.

2. (D) Except figure given below

All other are formed from two straight lines.

3. (B) No. of rectangles is 15.

4. (C) Monday falls on 1st, 8th, 15th, 22nd and 29th. So, 5th day from 21st which is 26th will be Friday.

5. (B) $15 \times 3 \div 15 + 5 - 2 = 5 + 15 - 10 = 10$

6. (A) People who can speak only one language is K + J + I

7. (A) Here, letters are coded by skipping letters in alphabetical order. The skipping pattern is 1, 2 and 3 letters. Hence, GATE is coded as HCWI.

8. (A) Only son of Vinay's grandfather is Vinay's father who is the father of Esha. So, Esha is the sister of Vinay.

9. (C) Adjacent faces of 1 are 2, 3, 5, and 6. So, the opposite face of 4 is 1.

10. (C) 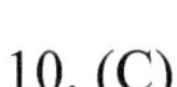 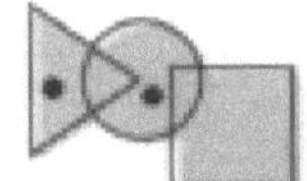

11. (C) Clearly, the right half of the sheet X is put on the left half. The combination of the design in left half and mirror image of the design in the right half will appear on the folded sheet.

12. (C) completes the figure matrix.

14. (C) Mirror Image of fig (X)

15. (C) Required no. is $16 \times 10 = 160$ (As first number is 10 times of second number).

16. (C) The solid in option (C) has 3 rectangular and 2 triangular faces.

17. (D) We have,

$$\frac{x-4}{3} - \frac{2x+1}{6} = \frac{5x+1}{2}$$

$$\frac{2x-8-2x-1}{6} = \frac{5x+1}{2}$$

$$15x = -12$$

$$x = -12/15 = -4/5$$

18. (B) 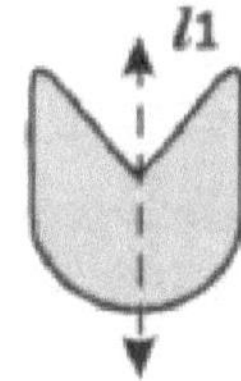

19. (A) Probability is 1/6

20. (A) $3x + 120° = 180°$ (sum of angles on straight line)
$x = 20°$

21. (C) Distance covered in 1 hour is 89.1/2.2 = 40.5 km

22. (C) $\angle B = \angle C$ (Base angles of an isosceles triangle are equal)

23. (C) We have
$(a^3 - 2a^2 + 4a - 5) - (-a^3 - 8a + 2a^2 + 5)$
$a^3 - 2a^2 + 4a - 5 + a^3 + 8a - 2a^2 - 5$
$2a^3 - 4a^2 + 12a - 10$

24. (B) Let sum be x
Amount in 10 years = $2x$
Interest in 10 years = x
R = 10% p.a.
According to question
Amount = $3x$, R = 10% p.a. T = ?, P = x, Interest = $2x$
T = 20 years

25. (B) Product of Means = Product of Extremes
$5p = 20$
$p = 4$

26. (D) Let maximum marks = x
% of marks required = 40%
Minimum marks = 40 + 40 = 80
40% of x = 80
$x = 200$

27. (A) No. of days = $\frac{120 \times 30}{150} = 24$
Time taken by them to complete remaining work is 24 days

28. (A) Let SP of 1 article = x
CP of 25 articles = SP of 20 articles
CP of 25 articles = $20x$
CP of 1 article = $20x/25 = 4x/5$
Gain = $x/5$
Gain% = $\frac{x/5}{4x/5} \times 100 = 25\%$

29. (B) $\angle DCE = \angle ACB = 106°$ (Vertically opposite angles); $\angle DCE = 106°$
$x + 48° + 106° = 180°$ (sum of angles of a triangle); $x = 26°$

30. (D) Let other integer be x
$x \times -6 = -48$
$x = 8$

31. (D) Let other number = x
$x \times \frac{-4}{3} = -\frac{9}{16}$
$x = \frac{-9}{16} \times -\frac{3}{4} = \frac{27}{64}$

32. (C) We have,
$3\frac{1}{12} - \left[1\frac{3}{4} + \left\{2\frac{1}{2} - \left(1\frac{1}{2} - \frac{1}{3}\right)\right\}\right]$
$\frac{37}{12} - \left[\frac{7}{4} + \left\{\frac{5}{2} - \left(\frac{3}{2} - \frac{1}{3}\right)\right\}\right]$
$\frac{37}{12} - \left[\frac{7}{4} + \left\{\frac{5}{2} - \frac{7}{6}\right\}\right]$
$\frac{37}{12} - \left[\frac{7}{4} + \frac{5}{2} - \frac{7}{6}\right] = \frac{37}{12} - \frac{37}{12} = 0$

33. (C) By Pythagoras theorem
$PQ^2 = PR^2 - QR^2$
$PQ^2 = 100 - 64$
$PQ = \sqrt{36}$
$PQ = 6$ cm

34. (D) Area of circular ring is 3850 m^2; Area of outer ring is 5544 m^2
Area of the path is Area of outer ring − Area of circular ring = 5544 – 3850 = 1694 m^2

35. (C) We have,

$$\left(5^3\right)^m \times \left(5^8\right)^m = 5^{72}$$

$$5^{3m} \times 5^{8m} = 5^{72}$$

$$5^{11m} = 5^{72}$$

$$11m = 72$$

$$m = 72/11 = 6\frac{6}{11}$$

36. (C) Length of lace required is 2 × 22/7 × 14 = 88 m

37. (C) Let Vishal's age = x years
His father's age = 44 years
According to question
$3x + 5 = 44$

38. (B) Time taken by her to read the book = $1\frac{3}{4} \times 6 = 7/4 \times 6 = 10\frac{1}{2}$ hours

39. (A) SP of recorder is 120/100 × 600 = ₹ 720

40. (D) Difference in their sum = 2500 – 2250 = ₹ 250
T = 3 years

$$R = \frac{45 \times 100}{250 \times 3} = 6\%$$

41. (B) Let population be x
% of children = (100 – 75) = 25%
25% of x = 20000
x = 80000
No. of women = 40/100 × 80000 = 32000

42. (A) Distance covered in 10 litres of petrol is 55.3 × 10 = 553 km

43. (B) Marks given for one correct answer = 4
So, Marks given for 9 correct answer = 4 × 9 = 36
Marks given for one incorrect answer = –2
So, marks given for 6 i.e. (15 – 9) incorrect answers = (–2) × 6 = –12
Manu's total score = 36 + (–12) = 24

44. (C) Time taken by him to complete the 500 m race is 13.5/100 × 500 = 67.5 secs

45. (C) Total pencils = $8y$
No. of children = 16
Each child get = $8y/16 = y/2$

46. (C) Area of rectangle = 30 × 20 = 600 cm²
Area of shaded parts = 2[1/2 × 10 × 15] = 150 cm²
Area of unshaded part = 600 – 150 = 450 cm²

47. (D) $\Delta AEC \cong \Delta ADB$ is true.

48. (B) We have,

$$= \frac{2 \times 3^4 \times 2^5}{3^2 \times \left(2^2\right)^2} = \frac{2 \times 2^5 \times 3^4}{3^2 \times 2^{2\times 2}}$$

$$= \frac{2^{1+5} \times 3^4}{2^4 \times 3^2} = \frac{2^6 \times 3^4}{2^4 \times 3^2} = 2^{6-4} \times 3^{4-2}$$

$$= 2^2 \times 3^2 = 4 \times 9 = 36$$

49. (D) Sum of the digits in the number is $11x + 30$

50. (B) If we multiply the second and third equations together, we obtain

$$x(y+1)y(x+1) = \frac{7}{9} \times \frac{5}{18}$$

$$\text{or } xy(y+1)(x+1) = \frac{35}{162}$$

From the first equation,

$$xy = \frac{1}{9}$$

$$\text{Therefore, } \frac{1}{9}(x+1)(y+1) = \frac{35}{162}$$

$$\text{or } (x+1)(y+1) = 9\left(\frac{35}{162}\right) = \frac{35}{18}$$

NATIONAL SCIENCE OLYMPIAD (NSO)

MOCK TEST PAPER – 1

ANSWERS									
1. (A)	2. (D)	3. (B)	4. (D)	5. (C)	6. (B)	7. (D)	8. (B)	9. (A)	10. (C)
11. (B)	12. (D)	13. (A)	14. (D)	15. (D)	16. (C)	17. (A)	18. (B)	19. (A)	20. (C)
21. (C)	22. (D)	23. (D)	24. (C)	25. (B)	26. (B)	27. (B)	28. (A)	29. (C)	30. (D)
31. (D)	32. (B)	33. (B)	34. (C)	35. (D)	36. (A)	37. (B)	38. (C)	39. (D)	40. (D)
41. (D)	42. (D)	43. (C)	44. (B)	45. (D)	46. (A)	47. (D)	48. (A)	49. (C)	50. (A)

1. (A) As North-East is 135° clockwise from West, in the same way North-West is 135° clockwise from South. Observe the image.

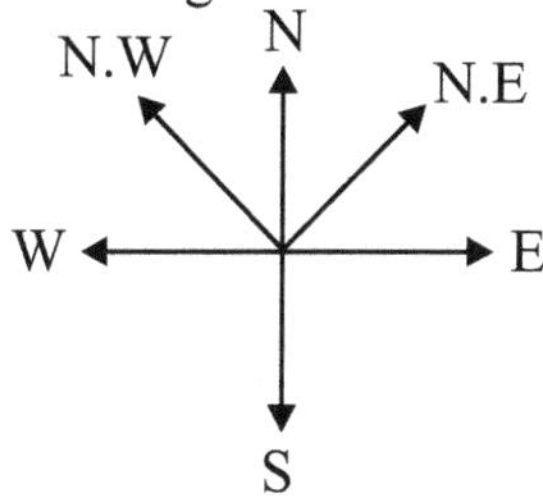

2. (D) When Kanika started she was facing North direction. Observe the image.

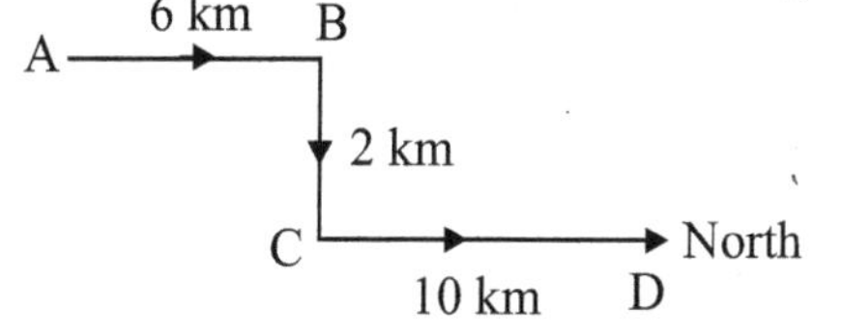

3. (B) As all the girls are beautiful but some of them are intelligent. Hence, some beautiful girls are intelligent.

4. (D) Required sum = $(70 - 5 \times 3)$ years = $(70 - 15)$ years = 55 years.

5. (C) Petals are the identification of flowers. Thorns are part of the stem of rose. It is not necessary that a flower always contains a stem, it can be plucked.

6. (B) The placement of the dot reflects the common region between triangle and the square. Among the given options only option B figure shows a common region between triangle and square only.

7. (D) The figures rotate anticlockwise at an angle and it is placed inside another figure with one more number of sides.

10. (C)

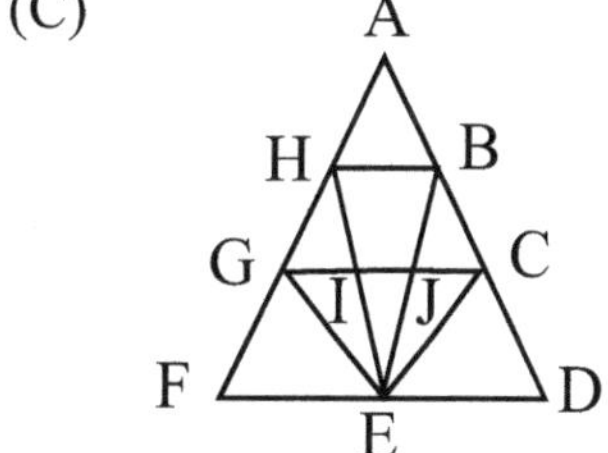

13. (A) The speed of light slows down after entering into water.

16. (C) This circuit is closed so it will allow the electricity to pass and glow the bulb

17. (A) The distance can be calculated as following:
Speed = 100 km/h = 100/60 km/min
Time = 17 hrs = 17×60 min
Distance = Speed $\times$ Time

$$= \frac{100 \times 17 \times 60}{60}$$

$= 1700$ km

18. (B) Due to constant velocity, the acceleration will be zero.

19. (A) It is clearly shown in the graph that B has travelled 20 m while A is still at the initial point and both bodies are moving with constant velocity, so A will always be 20 m behind B.

22. (D) All options are correctly matched with respect to excretory habits.

23. (D) Transpiration is the process of loss of water.

24. (C) Red blood cells contain haemoglobin which binds oxygen and transports it from one part to another part.

26. (B) Concentration of carbon dioxide in the exhaled air is higher than the inhaled air because various metabolic activities generate carbon dioxide. Concentration of nitrogen remains unchanged during breathing and concentration of oxygen reduces in the exhaled air.

28. (A) Goldfish feed upon the larva of mosquitoes. Thus, it will prevent the generation of mosquitoes. Spraying of oil and mosquito's repellent will cause many harms to the aquatic plant, so it is a bad option.

29. (C) Most of the water of the Earth is available in the form of ocean and sea which cannot be consumed due to high salinity. Fresh water in the form of lakes and rivers is limited.

35. (D)

36. (A) $Mg + O_2 \rightarrow \underset{\text{Magnesium oxide (ash)}}{MgO}$

$MgO + H_2O \rightarrow \underset{\text{Magnesium hydroxide (S)}}{Mg(OH)_2}$

Magnesium hydroxide is basic in nature, so it will turn red litmus into blue.

37. (B) Physical changes state about the change in the physical changes only.

39. (D) Lime fertilizers such as CaO are basic in nature, they reduce the acidity of the soil. Bee and ant stings are acidic, baking powder is basic. Toothpastes are alkaline which neutralizes the acidic action of the organic matter inside the mouth.

40. (D) Silver coating reflects the radiation.

41. (D) The heat gets trapped within the glass.

45. (D) Rhizobium shows symbiotic association with the legumes.

47. (D) There is soft iron rod placed inside the coil which will increase the electromagnetism.

49. (C) Cross pollination occurred in this plant species and the fertilization leads to the production of seeds.

MOCK TEST PAPER – 2

ANSWERS

1. (B)	2. (A)	3. (A)	4. (D)	5. (C)	6. (B)	7. (D)	8. (C)	9. (B)	10. (D)
11. (D)	12. (B)	13. (C)	14. (C)	15. (A)	16. (C)	17. (B)	18. (A)	19. (B)	20. (D)
21. (D)	22. (C)	23. (C)	24. (A)	25. (A)	26. (A)	27. (B)	28. (C)	29. (D)	30. (A)
31. (C)	32. (B)	33. (D)	34. (A)	35. (C)	36. (A)	37. (A)	38. (C)	39. (A)	40. (A)
41. (D)	42. (C)	43. (D)	44. (A)	45. (A)	46. (C)	47. (C)	48. (B)	49. (C)	50. (A)

1. (B) As the series continues, the already present element enlarges and a new element gets entry inside it and in the next step the outer shape or element is lost.

2. (A) Check the direction of dark end and hollow end.

5. (C) The figures 3, 6, 9 show the placement of two similar shapes one inside the other and the area between the two elements is shaded.
The figures 2, 4, 8 show the placement of one element inside a different element.
The figures 1, 5, 7 have two similar elements, one inside the other.

6. (B) One of the sons indicates that Manika's grandfather has more than one son, therefore Anil is uncle of Manika.

7. (D) The chronological arrangement is on the basis of the body parts from skull which is on the top of the body up to heel, bottom most part of the body.

8. (C) The alphabets refer to the initials of the names of each kid.

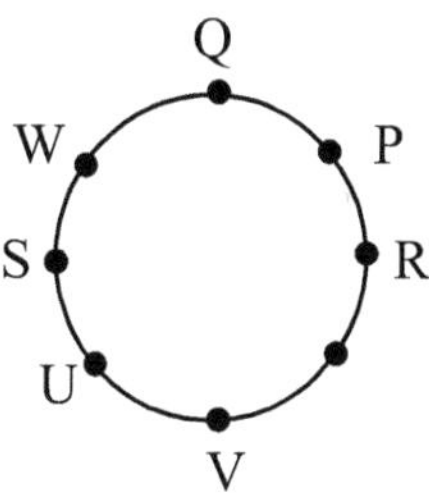

9. (B) S1 tells about the causes of the S2 action. So, the Britishers had to leave our nation.

10. (D) All the three are different occupations.

11. (D) The presence of fungus on the bread characterises the decayed form of bread. The saprophytic nutrition is the type when the organisms obtain their food from the decaying matters. Most of the fungi are saprotrophs.

12. (B) Polysaccharides are the main constituents of potatoes in the form of starch. In the mouth, food is first mixed with the saliva, salivary amylase present in saliva converts starch into some simple sugars. Pancreatic amylases found in the small intestine converts remaining starch into simpler sugars

such as disaccharides. Disaccharides are found in the small intestine which completely breaks down the disaccharides.

13. (C) Sericin is that gummy substance that holds the two strands of fibroin of a silk fibre together.

14. (C) Cashmere goat is used for Cashmere wool. Silk is a protein fibre.

15. (A) When a liquid is heated, the temperature of the liquid increases, hence the average kinetic energy also increases.

16. (C) The bulb of the thermometer absorbs the heat, so it is not held by that side.

17. (B) Baking soda is bitter in taste as it is a base. Acids taste sour while bases taste bitter.

18. (A) To neutralize the basicity of the organic farms, some organic matters should be added by F1 and to decrease the acidity increased in the farms because of chemical fertilizers F2 should use some bases such as quick lime.

19. (B) $CH_3COOH + NaHCO_3 \rightarrow$

$CH_3COONa + \underset{X}{CO_2} + H_2O$

$\underset{X}{CO_2} + Ca(OH)_2 \rightarrow \underset{\text{Calcium carbonate}}{CaCO_3} + H_2O$

20. (D) When sugar is dissolved, the sugar changes its physical state, hence physical change occurs. On heating the sugar decomposes into carbon and water, these changes come under chemical and irreversible changes.

22. (C) Penguins huddle together but polar bear prefers solitaire life.

24. (A) Rotation of the Earth causes the difference in the pressure.

26. (A) As trees prevent the soil erosion, so a large number of trees will result into the more soil conservation.

30. (A) Bronchial respiration refers to the involvement of bronchioles (In Mammals), cutaneous respiration is respiration through skin (In Amphibians), insects breathe through trachea and gills support the exchange of oxygen under water (In Fish).

32. (B) Urine formation takes place in kidney, it is then passed to ureter which transfers to bladder and it is excreted by the urethra.

37. (A) The acceleration (a) can be calculated as the following.

$$a = \frac{\text{Final velocity} - \text{Initial velocity}}{\text{change in time}}$$

$$= \frac{40-0}{10}$$

$$= 4 \text{ ms}^{-2}$$

38. (C) Oscillation of the pendulum is constant irrespective of weight and length.

41. (D) The strength of magnetic field of a coil and strength of the current flowing through it is directly proportional to each other.

42. (C) The power of the bulb is 60 W.

43. (D) Lateral inversion refers to the apparent sideways inversion.

44. (A) Dispersion refers to the splitting of light into different colours, it occurs after the process of refraction and total internal reflection.

45. (A) Such light retraces, and it coincides with the normal incidence of light, hence the angle of curvature is zero.

46. (C) Increased Buzzard population will decrease the population of mouse, which will increase the population of Plantain.

47. (C) The heat of the boiling water will make the movement of the air molecules fast and will allow it to cover more space in short time. This property will cause the inflation of the balloon.

50. (A) Relation between °C and °F is as follows:

$$\frac{C}{100} = \frac{F-32}{180}$$

NATIONAL CYBER OLYMPIAD (NCO)

MOCK TEST PAPER – 1

ANSWERS									
1. (C)	2. (A)	3. (C)	4. (D)	5. (C)	6. (A)	7. (B)	8. (B)	9. (A)	10. (C)
11. (C)	12. (B)	13. (A)	14. (C)	15. (B)	16. (A)	17. (A)	18. (C)	19. (B)	20. (B)
21. (C)	22. (C)	23. (B)	24. (A)	25. (C)	26. (B)	27. (D)	28. (A)	29. (D)	30. (A)
31. (D)	32. (C)	33. (C)	34. (A)	35. (C)	36. (D)	37. (C)	38. (A)	39. (C)	40. (D)
41. (C)	42. (A)	43. (A)	44. (B)	45. (D)	46. (B)	47. (C)	48. (C)	49. (C)	50. (A)

1. (C) Total students are 12 + Maya + 27 = 40

2. (A)

$A \xrightarrow{+7} H$

$G \xrightarrow{+7} N$

$F \xrightarrow{+7} M$

Similarly, $L \xrightarrow{+7} S$

3. (C) We have,
14 N 10 L 42 P 2 M 8
$14 \times 10 + 42 \div 2 - 8 = 140 + 21 - 8 = 153$

4. (D) The pattern is : 13 + 15 = 28, 36 + 54 = 90. Then 45 + 63 = 108

5. (C) 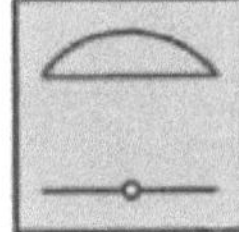

6. (A)

7. (B) 

All mothers are women and some mothers and some women may be doctors.

8. (B) In the given code for the word 'LATEST' each letter is alternately decreased or increased by 3. Hence, the code for the word 'PAPERS' is MDMHOV.

9. (A) Mirror Image of the given figure (X)

10. (C) No. of squares is 12.

11. (C) Merge Cells

12. (B) Personalization

13. (A) It is used to merge the content of multiple cells into one and align it to center.

14. (C) Macros

15. (B) Homegroup

16. (A) Ctrl + Shift + >

17. (A) Hotspots

18. (C) Option (A) is of Insert Cells. Option (B) is of Format Cells. Option (D) is of Merge and Center.

19. (B) It is used for wrapping text by displaying it on multiple lines.

20. (B) Speech Synthesizer

21. (C) Active Cell

22. (C) Inkjet printer

23. (B) 

24. (A) Differential analyser is a mechanical analogue computer designed to solve differential equations by integration.

25. (C) Orientation option

26. (B) Intel 4004

27. (D) Microprocessor

28. (A) Homegroup is a home network feature in Windows 7 that allow to share files and printer among connected computers.

29. (D)

30. (A) Device Stage

31. (D) Breadcrumb trail

32. (C) Macros

33. (C) By pressing control Z, one can undo last actions.

34. (A) Ctrl + K, is used to insert or modify a hyperlink.

35. (C) Laser pointers

36. (D) Slide Master

37. (C) Effects of theme can also be changed like colors and fonts.

38. (A) All Excel formulas begin with an equal sign.

39. (C) a-(ii), b-(iv), c-(i), d-(iii)

40. (D) It is used to align the text to left.

41. (C) 14

42. (A) $A = B - P^\wedge 3 / (C^\wedge 2 * B) + Q * R + T$

43. (A) You made an invalid choice

44. (B) URL

45. (D) Except Television rest all are latest technologies.

46. (B) a-(iv), b-(i), c-(ii), d-(iii)

47. (C) Static RAM

48. (C) FLOPS and MIPS are units of measure for the numerical computing performance of a computer.

49. (C) Air Print

50. (A) VR headsets

MOCK TEST PAPER – 2

ANSWERS									
1. (B)	2. (D)	3. (A)	4. (C)	5. (D)	6. (D)	7. (A)	8. (A)	9. (A)	10. (D)
11. (C)	12. (C)	13. (B)	14. (B)	15. (C)	16. (B)	17. (C)	18. (D)	19. (C)	20. (A)
21. (D)	22. (C)	23. (A)	24. (C)	25. (C)	26. (A)	27. (B)	28. (D)	29. (A)	30. (A)
31. (D)	32. (D)	33. (A)	34. (B)	35. (C)	36. (A)	37. (C)	38. (D)	39. (C)	40. (A)
41. (C)	42. (A)	43. (B)	44. (B)	45. (A)	46. (D)	47. (B)	48. (D)	49. (A)	50. (B)

1. (B) As per the code for the word GOLD and LIVE

G	O	L	D	I	V	E
5	1	2	4	9	8	3

Hence the code for word VOID is 8194

2. (D)

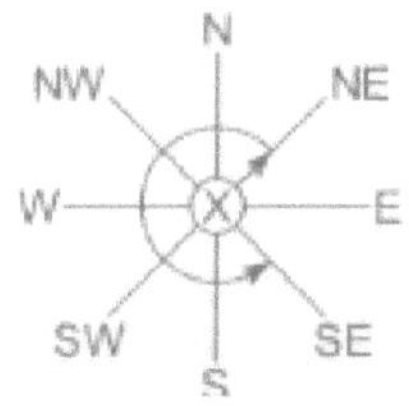

Monika is facing South-East now.

3. (A)

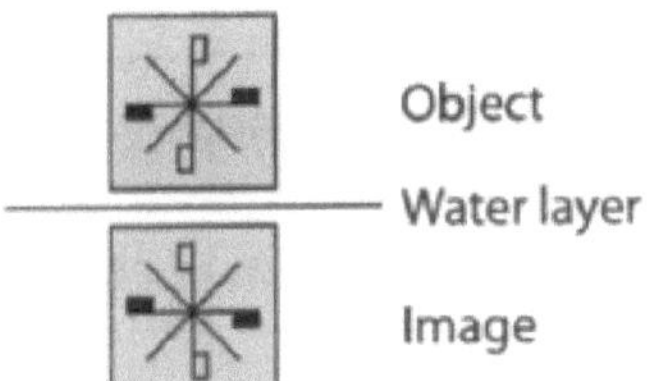

4. (C) Here, the pattern followed is

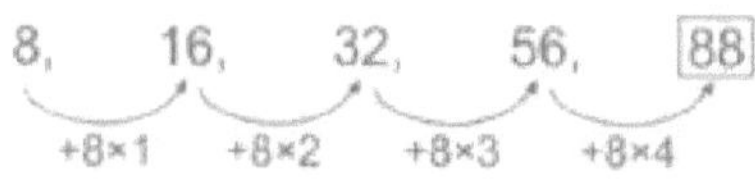

5. (D) WET cannot be formed as T is not present in the given letter.

6. (D) The mother of Abhay's father is Abhay's paternal grandmother, who is wife of maternal grandfather of Prerna, i.e., Prerna's maternal grandmother. So, Prerna is cousin of Abhay.

7. (A) Adjacent faces of 1 are 2, 3, 5, and 6. So, the opposite face of 4 is 1.

8. (A) 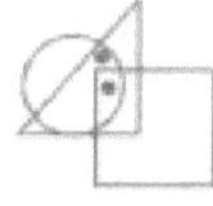

9. (A) 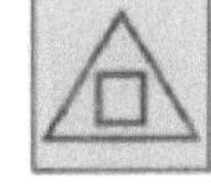

10. (D) 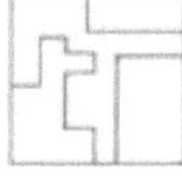

11. (C) Flatbed

12. (C) Web browser

13. (B) Shift + Space

14. (B) Bit

15. (C) Intel Core i7

16. (B) Cells Styles

17. (C) spreadsheet

18. (D) Insert a hyperlink – Alt + K. Shortcut to insert hyperlink is Ctrl + K

19. (C) Disk defragmenter

20. (A) It is used to rotate text diagonally or vertically.

21. (D) Except car rest all are latest technology in IT.

22. (C) Agri bot

24. (C) HoloLens

25. (C) Spyware

26. (A) Fiber optic

27. (B) Web portal

28. (D) Web servers are not only used for serving the World Wide Web. They can also be found embedded in devices such as printers, routers, webcams and serving only a local network.

30. (A) Barcode reader

31. (D) Hard disk is secondary storage device and rest all are primary storage devices.

32. (D) 2010

33. (A) a-(iii), b-(iv), c-(ii), d-(i)

34. (B) LINE command

35. (C) $A = B + P^2 / (C * B) - Q * R + T$

36. (A) FTP

37. (C) Ctrl + ;

38. (D) 

39. (C)

40. (A) Handout master

41. (C) Ctrl + Alt + S

42. (A) Hyphenation

43. (B) Sync Center

44. (B) Performance
45. (A) Memory card
46. (D) a-(ii), b-(i), c-(iii), d-(iv)
47. (B) BIOS
48. (D) Early public web portals were AOL, Excite, Netvibes, iGoogle, MSN, Naver, Lycos, Prodigy, Indiatimes, Rediff, and Yahoo!.
49. (A) a-(iii), b-(iv), c-(ii), d-(i)
50. (B) a-(iv), b-(i), c-(ii), d-(iii)

INTERNATIONAL ENGLISH OLYMPIAD (IEO)

MOCK TEST PAPER – 1

ANSWERS									
1. (C)	2. (A)	3. (D)	4. (A)	5. (B)	6. (C)	7. (B)	8. (A)	9. (D)	10. (C)
11. (B)	12. (D)	13. (A)	14. (B)	15. (B)	16. (D)	17. (C)	18. (B)	19. (C)	20. (A)
21. (B)	22. (D)	23. (C)	24. (A)	25. (B)	26. (B)	27. (D)	28. (B)	29. (C)	30. (D)
31. (D)	32. (C)	33. (A)	34. (B)	35. (C)	36. (A)	37. (A)	38. (C)	39. (A)	40. (B)
41. (D)	42. (B)	43. (C)	44. (C)	45. (D)	46. (A)	47. (D)	48. (C)	49. (C)	50. (B)

1. (C) Predominant is the synonym of important.
2. (A) As forbid is the synonym of prohibit in the same way courage is the synonym of valour.
3. (D) Gallant is an adjective, stands for the bold, courageous person. Discourteous, impolite and coward are the antonyms of gallant.
4. (A) Independent person is self-dependent and self-sufficient. Maverick, free and self-reliant are the synonyms o independent. Self-conscious stands for uneasy person.
8. (A) Homophones are the words which have similar pronunciation.
9. (D) Hatch is a type of door and hatch is the locking of the door.
11. (B) Plenty of stands for the amount or degree of enough or more than enough.
16. (D) No article is placed before the name.
18. (B) Phrasal verb is the combination of verb with any other word, it may be noun, pronoun, adjective or even verb.
19. (C) Proverbs reflect an advice or lesson other than its original meaning.
28. (B) I might score highest in the class this year.
Might is used in the case of possibility or probability.
29. (C) Punctuating of the sentence requires the capitalization of the words and placing the suitable punctuating marks.

31. (D) It is an informative notice as the information of the competition is displayed.

36. (A) Capitalization of the alphabets is also a part of correct punctuation. Placing of comma is required before and after the description.

46. (A) When 'can' is converted into indirect form, it gets converted into 'could'.

47. (D) 'Am' is always used as the helping verb for 'I'. In the case of confusion, whether and or pair is used as the conjunction.

48. (C) 'the tip of the iceberg' is used in the situation when the small problem of the situation is visible, but the biggest part is still hidden.

50. (B) 'Handed in' refers to the submitting something.

MOCK TEST PAPER – 2

ANSWERS									
1. (B)	2. (D)	3. (D)	4. (A)	5. (C)	6. (B)	7. (D)	8. (C)	9. (D)	10. (A)
11. (A)	12. (B)	13. (C)	14. (B)	15. (D)	16. (D)	17. (D)	18. (C)	19. (C)	20. (C)
21. (B)	22. (D)	23. (A)	24. (C)	25. (A)	26. (B)	27. (C)	28. (A)	29. (C)	30. (B)
31. (C)	32. (A)	33. (D)	34. (A)	35. (B)	36. (C)	37. (A)	38. (D)	39. (C)	40. (C)
41. (B)	42. (A)	43. (D)	44. (A)	45. (B)	46. (D)	47. (D)	48. (C)	49. (B)	50. (A)

2. (D) Necessary capitalization of the words and putting the appropriate punctuation marks are required to correct a sentence. The Tsunami is a noun, so the capitalization is necessary.

3. (D) The complete sentence is as follows: I need not go to market to buy things for me, my mother does it for me.

12. (B) Proverb is the piece of sentence which refers to the advise or advice or some kind of truth in the direct form of words.

13. (C) Phrasal verb is the combination of two words.

15. (D) no article is placed before any proper noun.

16. (D) gorgeous is observation type of adjective, black is colour adjective, new is age adjective. Wooden, plastic and silk are material adjective. Tiny, huge and giant are size adjective and circular oval and rectangular are shape adjective.

19. (C) Reciprocal pronoun shows mutual relationship. Each other is also an such pronoun but is used to show mutualism between two persons while one another is used for a group of more than two persons.

20. (C) Abstract noun refers to the feeling which have no physical existence. Rustle and patter are the sounds of rustle and patter.

23. (A) Homophones are the words which have same pronunciation but different spellings and meanings.

Advice is guidance, advise is recommendation

24. (C) Adventure refers to the physical activity which involves some danger.

26. (B) Antiseptic covers all the range of microorganisms. Antibacterial are specific for bacteria while antifungal is specific for fungi. Analgesics are the pain killers.

27. (C) Disease is the alteration in the normal body functions. Infection, allergy, injury and disorder are the types of disease while syndrome is a group of diseases.

28. (A) Antonym of condemn is acquit. Meaning of condemn is attack or criticize.

29. (C) Diligent is the synonym of hardworking.

32. (A) Advisor stands for the person who advices in any particular field.

34. (A) Writer's sister is elder to her. He wished her good luck for his chosen career path while he is still waiting to write his board exams.

35. (B) Taking liberty stand for the work done without the permission or done without caring of others. As the writer of the letter is about to write his exams so he wrote 'I can't take liberty' because he cared for his studies.

37. (A) Noble prize is a very prestigious prize in the world.

41. (B) Exclamatory mark is placed after the exclamatory word.

47. (D) The complete sentence is as following. The streets were full of water because it had been raining continuously since past 10 hours.

48. (C) Participle prepositions have endings with -ed or -ing.

9 789357 942324

Printed by Libri Plureos GmbH in Hamburg,
Germany